Exercise Book for

Working With Words

A Handbook for Media Writers and Editors

FIFTH EDITION

Brian S. Brooks
University of Missouri – Columbia

James L. Pinson
Eastern Michigan University

Jean Gaddy Wilson
Weiner, Edrich, Brown, Inc.

Bedford / St. Martin's
Boston ◆ New York

For information, write: Bedford/St. Martin's, 75 Arlington Street, Boston, MA 02116   (617-399-4000)

ISBN: 0–312–39890-5

Preface

Learning any skill can't be done simply by reading about it. Skills have to be practiced. That's what this workbook helps students do, whether on their own or as part of classwork.

From years spent working as copy editors and journalism teachers, we've seen the kinds of mistakes often made by students and professionals. We've drawn on that experience and created these exercises to help students recognize and avoid the most common pitfalls. This workbook enables students to master the language skills required to become — and to excel as — reporters or editors in print, broadcast or online media.

We've organized the exercises to follow the presentation in the fifth edition of *Working With Words*. These exercises cover grammar, usage, spelling, tightening, wire-service style and copy editing. They also reinforce skills needed to write with objectivity and sensitivity and to write for different media.

When considering a new topic, we often start with short-answer questions to help students summarize the main points regarding that topic. Then we provide practical exercises focusing on specific difficulties. And finally, we offer exercises that review the material, so that students get the benefit of repetition, which is necessary for retention.

Students should be warned not to try to do these exercises "by ear." Those who don't read the relevant information in the text will probably score poorly. That's because we've chosen to focus primarily on those points that typically trouble students the most—when the rules of written English differ from how most people actually speak.

We also suggest that students read the relevant section of the textbook before tackling an exercise so they'll have a general idea of the issues involved. Then, they can try doing the exercise with the textbook open, looking up any issues that confuse them.

If students have difficulty finding an answer in the text, they can look in the index at the back of the book and then, if necessary, in a wire-service style manual.

Brian S. Brooks
James L. Pinson
Jean Gaddy Wilson

Contents

Basic Skills Pretest

Name: ______________________

Class: ______________________

Date: ______________________

This test focuses on your knowledge of the requirements of correct sentence structure, subject-predicate agreement, pronoun-antecedent agreement, pronoun case, principal parts of verbs, punctuation and a few common spelling and usage errors.

A. Label each of the following *S* for sentence, *F* for fragment, *R* for run-on, *FU* for fused or *CS* for comma-splice sentence.

_____**1.** The assailant fled on foot, he is described as white, about 6 feet tall, 180 pounds and wearing a black leather jacket.

_____**2.** Several people make reproductions of high-wheeled, antique bicycles, but original bikes are hard to find.

_____**3.** A ring of flames shot up onstage, and standing in their midst, Garth Brooks played guitar and sang.

_____**4.** The Internet provider will offer accounts to individuals businesses may sign up, too.

_____**5.** The taxi commission in New York is asking the city's cabdrivers—world famous for rudeness—to be polite and is teaching them, many of them foreigners who speak little English, 50 expressions, such as "Thank you for hailing me, madam; I'd be happy to take you to Brooklyn," and "I'll do my best to avoid the potholes," but the exercise is receiving more jokes than praise.

_____**6.** Even the president.

_____**7.** About 67 percent of teen-age girls have sex but only because boys pressure them, according to a Seventeen magazine survey.

_____**8.** The Humane Society of Springfield is sponsoring a pet walkathon Sunday, walkers need not bring a pet to participate.

_____**9.** Dan Blausley pitched a no-hitter for Summerfield on Tuesday the team won 3-1 over Amantee.

_____**10.** According to the St. John's County, Fla., ordinance against nude dancing, the *buttocks* is defined as "the area at the rear of the human body (sometimes referred to as the gluteus maximus) which lies between two imaginary lines running parallel to the ground when a person is standing, the first or top of such lines being one-half inch below the top of the vertical cleavage of the nates (i.e., the prominence formed by the muscles running from the back of the hip to the back of the leg) and the second or bottom line being one-half inch above the lowest point of the curvature of the fleshy protuberance (sometimes referred to as the gluteal fold), and between two imaginary lines, one on each side of the body."

B. Circle the correct answers.

1. One of the three never (miss, misses) a deadline.

2. None of the contractors (has, have) bid on the contract.

3. Each (was, were) given a choice of seats.

4. A Microsoft Xbox, along with a controller, (sell, sells) for about $199.

5. Forsyth said, "(A lot, Alot, Allot) of us don't know what he's doing."

6. The media (were, was) out in full.

7. The five-member council filed (its, their) report this morning.

8. He lectured on the evils of communism to (whoever, whomever) would listen.

9. Is this briefcase (your's, yours)?

10. But who founded the company? It was (she, her).

11. Bennington said he doubted anyone could find a happier person than (he, him).

12. (There are, There's) two to help out with farm chores now.

13. (Who's, Whose) sorry now?

14. (Us, We) citizens should have more say in it.

15. Neither of the criticisms has lost (its, it's, their) sting.

16. She said she felt (bad, badly) about missing the meeting.

17. He is the (younger, youngest) of the three brothers.

18. This is where the (Petersens', Petersen's, Petersens) live.

19. That's (she, her).

20. Between you and (I, me), nothing could be further from the truth.

21. Give the information to Steve or (me, myself).

22. The City Council will hold (its, their) next meeting Monday.

23. A reporter should check (his, his or her, their) copy.

24. (Who, Whom) did he say was the best photographer he has?

25. Most surveyed said Cola A goes down (more smoothly, smoother) than Cola B.

26. The perfume smells (sweet, sweetly).

27. What will the (affect, effect) be?

28. She said the plan worked (good, well).

29. He had just (laid, layed, lain, lied) it down.

30. Johnson told him to (set, sit) down and rest his feet.

31. Her mother asked her to (raise, rise) up for a second.

32. She said, "I think (you're, your) sitting on my newspaper."

33. (Among, Between) the three of them, he said, they'll come up with something.

C. Circle the correct answers. Some sentences require more than one circle.

1. She is one of those people (who, whom) (is, are) never too busy to see a student.

2. Guess (who's, whose) coming to Pine Knob this week.

3. (Prior to, Before) the operation, she was in constant pain.

4. (While, Although) the panel (disagree, disagrees) with each other now, at one time that wasn't the case.

5. They said they hoped to put together a proposal that (will, would) compare favorably (to, with) the one (that, which) has been submitted by Frech Corp.

6. She said she didn't know (if, whether, whether or not) she would go out for basketball next year after this losing season.

7. He was (convinced, persuaded) that he should try to (convince, persuade) others to go to the seminar.

8. Several of them plan to return to meet with (each other, one another).

9. They said they thought (she, her) to be (she, her).

10. They said they thought (she, her) was (she, her).

11. (We, Us) journalism students have it rough but not (as, so) rough as (they, them).

12. It is (she, her), not (he, him), of (who, whom) the family speaks.

13. He had just (laid, lay, layed, lain) down when the phone (rang, rung).

14. The budget (composes, comprises, is comprised of, is constituted of) six parts.

15. His vase was different (from, than) the one at the museum; compared (to, with) his, the museum's looked plain.

16. "What a (prejudice, prejudiced) thing to say!" she said.

17. Every reporter and editor did (her, his, his or her, their) part in getting out this special election edition.

18. For JoAnn and (me, myself), good night.

19. If the river (raises, rises) another foot, the road will flood.

20. The new father looked (proud, proudly) as he left the hospital with his wife and new daughter.

21. The car ran (good, well) after she gave it a tuneup.

22. Preston said nobody seems to know (who, whom) to call for information.

23. He (presently, currently) pitches for the Toledo Mudhens.

24. One thing (lead, led) to another.

25. She said she'd like to examine the issue (farther, further).

26. What does he think will be the (affect, effect) of the law?

27. That's not the way it's (suppose, supposed) to be.

28. I (use, used) to enjoy skiing until I broke my leg.

D. To the left of each number, put the letter of the sentence that is punctuated correctly.

_____ 1. a. Fans at Sheridan, Westfield and Hamilton Heights supported the multiclass tournament.
b. Fans at Sheridan, Westfield, and Hamilton Heights supported the multiclass tournament.

_____ 2. a. Kansas City, Mo. is on the Kansas side of the state.
b. Kansas City, Mo., is on the Kansas side of the state.

_____ 3. a. Still, he was enthusiastic when three schools — Cherry Tree, Carmel Junior High and Carmel High School — applied for the Indiana 2005 grant.
b. Still, he was enthusiastic when three schools, Cherry Tree, Carmel Junior High, and Carmel High School, applied for the Indiana 2005 grant.

_____ 4. a. Miller Co., Inc., and its employees have signed a new contract.
b. Miller Co. Inc. and its employees have signed a new contract.

_____ 5. **a.** He said, "Our plate is pretty full with issues of rapid growth."
b. He said, "Our plate is pretty full with issues of rapid growth".

_____ 6. **a.** He said two of his favorite movies—"Claire's Knee" and "Chloe in the Afternoon"—are by director, Eric Rohmer.
b. He said two of his favorite movies—"Claire's Knee" and "Chloe in the Afternoon"—are by director Eric Rohmer.

_____ 7. **a.** The Fenders' daughter Rosa will be married in June and their other daughter, Vanessa, in July.
b. The Fenders' daughter, Rosa, will be married in June and their other daughter Vanessa in July.

_____ 8. **a.** "Who's there?" she screamed.
b. "Who's there?", she screamed.

_____ 9. **a.** The superintendent said: "We can't afford everything. We have to pick and choose."
b. The superintendent said, "We can't afford everything. We have to pick and choose."

_____ 10. **a.** A large flowery couch sat on the front porch.
b. A large, flowery couch sat on the front porch.

_____ 11. **a.** She said her courses made her a well-prepared job applicant.
b. She said her courses made her a well prepared job applicant.

_____ 12. **a.** The 21-year-old pool has problems; and it could cost nearly half a million dollars to bring it up to state codes.
b. The 21-year-old pool has problems, and it could cost nearly half a million dollars to bring it up to state codes.

_____ 13. **a.** Shoemaker, however says she won't file suit.
b. Shoemaker, however, says she won't file suit.

_____ 14. **a.** Rain's in the forecast for the rest of the week, too.
b. Rain's in the forecast for the rest of the week too.

_____ 15. **a.** He said he didn't do it then, but should have.
b. He said he didn't do it then but should have.

Name: _____

Class: _____

Date: _____

A. Use the correct copy-editing symbols to make the requested changes.

1. Insert the letter *s* after the *n* in this word: inert.

2. Insert the word *not* between these words: will always.

3. Delete the last *e* in the first word, and close the space as needed: employeee benefits.

4. Delete the third *e* from the first word, and close the space as needed: employeee benefits.

5. Delete the word *very,* and close the space: not very tall.

6. Delete the extra *n,* and make this one word: cannnot.

7. Transpose the *s* and the second *e:* thees.

8. Transpose the abbreviation and year in this date: 67 A.D.

9. Abbreviate *United States* Army in this sentence.

10. Make this numeral a number written out: 17.

11. Mark this sentence—including the number in front of it—so that it will be indented as a paragraph.

12. Mark this sentence—including the number in front of it—so that it will become part of the same paragraph as No. 11.

B. Use copy-editing symbols to edit the following news brief for wire-service style, spelling and any other errors.

A Rio loma man bitten by a poisonus corral snake bit back.

Richard Douglass, 44, was wakling along United State Hiway Forty-Four near Rountree when he stopped to pick up something he thuoght he saw in the gras but a poisonous snate but hishand.

Douglass bit the snakes head off, then saved his own life by using the reptiles skin for a tournicut to to keep the venem from spreding.

Douglas ought to fully recover, because the venem's pread was stopped intime, said Susie Chavez, a spokesman for springfield Hospital.

Grammar Basics

Name: _____

Class: _____

Date: _____

Short Answer

1. What are some of the differences between spoken and written English?

2. Why do journalists use traditional grammar rather than one of the newer grammars, such as structural or transformational?

3. Why is consistency such a concern in the publishing industry?

4. List the eight parts of speech.

5. What are the three verbals?

6. List at least five parts of a sentence.

7. What is the difference between the parts of speech and the parts of a sentence?

CHAPTER 1

Grammar Basics

Name [illegible]

Class [illegible]

Short Answer

1. What are [illegible] differences [illegible] spoken [illegible]

2. Why [illegible] sentences [illegible] rather than [illegible] such as [illegible]

3. Why [illegible] part of speech [illegible]

4. [illegible] eight parts [illegible]

5. What [illegible]

6. [illegible] least two parts of a sentence [illegible]

7. What is the difference between the part of speech and the [illegible]

Name: _____

Class: _____

Date: _____

Talking Shop

Identifying Parts of Speech

A. Beside each group of words, label what part of speech the words would typically be.

_____ **1.** was   says   edits   reads

_____ **2.** gee   ouch   oops   whew

_____ **3.** smart   handsome   wicked   sexy

_____ **4.** barn   car   television   magazine

_____ **5.** very   cautiously   quite   softly

_____ **6.** and   but   because   or

_____ **7.** she   their   you   us

_____ **8.** by   on   under   before

B. Above the following sentences, adapted from an AP story, label each word by its part of speech: *N* for noun, *P* for pronoun, *V* for verb, *Adj.* for adjective, *Adv.* for adverb, *I* for interjection, *C* for conjunction or *Prep.* for preposition.

Remember that many words can be used as different parts of speech. Label the part of speech the word is in the sentence here. Also, if the word is normally a noun, for example, but is being used here as an adjective, label it *N/Adj.*

If you have difficulty, look the word up in the dictionary. If the word can be different parts of speech, look for an example of a sentence in the dictionary close to the one here.

1. The Postal Service is considering ending the practice of delivering mail "postage due" when the stamps on a letter or package are insufficient.

2. Instead, underpaid mail would be returned to the sender, just as is done currently with mail lacking any stamp.

3. Postal officials said the change is necessary because with all the families with two income earners or only one parent, mail carriers are often unable to find anyone home these days to pay the postage due.

Identifying Verbals

In the space before each of the following sentences, identify the italicized word. If it's used as part of the verb, put V in front of the sentence. If it's used as a participle, put P. If it's used as a gerund, put G. If it's used as an infinitive, put I.

Then, after the comma, label the part of speech for which the italicized word or the phrase containing it is substituting.

(Hint: A verb would be serving as a main verb. A participle would be substituting for an adjective, a gerund for a noun. An infinitive, however, could be substituting for a noun, an adjective or an adverb, depending on the sentence.)

____,_____ **1.** She loves *playing* the violin.

____,_____ **2.** *Playing* the violin, she seemed a natural.

____,_____ **3.** She was *playing* the violin.

____,_____ **4.** It seems that everybody is *jogging* these days.

____,_____ **5.** *To ask* too many questions is dangerous.

____,_____ **6.** *Looking* out the window, he saw troops in the street.

____,_____ **7.** The protesters asked the president *to step* down.

____,_____ **8.** *Riding* her pony was how she spent most of her time.

____,_____ **9.** You'd have to be awfully lucky *to win*.

____,_____ **10.** The contractor asked the Planning and Zoning Commission for permission *to build* on the property.

____,_____ **11.** Miller has been *writing* a novel for three years.

____,_____ **12.** Debaters like *arguing*.

____,_____ **13.** The candidates *debating* tonight are all independents.

____,_____ **14.** The couple downstairs did nothing but *fight*. (Hint: The word *to* is implied.)

____,_____ **15.** The minister said she felt *chosen* by God.

____,_____ **16.** *Working* story problems in math was not his idea of a good time.

____,_____ **17.** He asked her *to write* him often.

____,_____ **18.** Her team *having* lost in the playoffs, she didn't watch the Stanley Cup finals.

____,_____ **19.** We have plenty of food *to eat*.

____,_____ **20.** The film star said her life was *acting*.

_____,_____ **21.** She *was driving* fast.

_____,_____ **22.** She *loves* driving fast.

_____,_____ **23.** She loves *to drive* fast.

_____,_____ **24.** *Driving* too fast, she lost control of the car.

_____,_____ **25.** The driver *having gone* too fast, an accident was likely.

Identifying Parts of a Sentence

A. Underline the complete subject of the following sentences once, the complete predicate twice. Then, circle the simple subject, and put a square around the simple predicate. If a sentence has more than one clause, label the parts of each clause.

1. The professor gave easy tests.

2. The professor was tough, but he was fair.

3. The professor and his assistant entertained and inspired students.

4. The distinguished-looking, gray-haired professor lectured entertainingly but gave difficult tests.

B. Label the various kinds of grammatical objects in these sentences.
    DO—direct object
    IO—indirect object
    O of Inf—object of infinitive
    O of Part—object of participle
    O of Prep—object of preposition
    O of Gerund—object of gerund

1. She sent her husband flowers for his birthday.

2. Would you hand me those, Paul?

3. Sammy Sosa slammed the ball out of the park.

4. They thought him to be headed for jail.

5. Hurdling the fence, he outpaced the pack.

6. Reporting news is no job for the bashful.

C. Circle the predicate adjectives in these sentences, and put squares around the predicate nominatives.

1. I'm tired, but you look good.

2. Yes, I feel fine.

3. Ben was there.

4. Joan, the guide, seems well-informed.

5. That's Joan, our tour guide.

6. It is I.

7. The package was due any day.

8. It's been proved. It's proven. It's a proven fact.

9. It's nice to see you.

10. It's been a while.

D. Put *A* in front of the sentence if the italicized word is an appositive, *N* if a noun of direct address or *P* if a predicate objective.

_____**1.** *Hank,* would you hand me that coffee cup?

_____**2.** The dog, *Fido,* is just a pup.

_____**3.** The nurse, Ursula, sang the baby, Jenny, a song, *Bill.*

_____**4.** His friends called him *Biff.*

_____**5.** My sons, *Andrew and Taylor,* love watching cartoons.

Quick Start: A Checklist of Common Mistakes

A. Circle the correct answers. Some sentences require more than one circle.

1. The Taliban had blown up (a, an) historic religious site in the area.

2. (A lot of, Alot of, Many) refugees fled across the border.

3. The press secretary said matters were running (smooth, smoothly).

4. The committee (adopted, passed) a resolution calling for a local day honoring the homeless.

5. Critics said no one could be sure of the measure's long-term (affect, effect).

6. Hart (allegedly raped the woman, was charged with rape).

7. They couldn't agree (among, between) the three of them.

8. (As, Like) a wise man once said, "It ain't over till it's over."

9. She's doing better in the polls than (he, him).

10. The victim was described as a woman in her early 20s with (blond, blonde) hair.

11. The dispute centers (around, on) Kashmir.

12. That's what he said: (he, He) wouldn't surrender.

13. In the following sentence, there (should, should not) be a comma before the word *and:*

    "The vice president attended the Cabinet meeting and then flew to Colorado."

14. The senator compared Saddam Hussein (to, with) Adolf Hitler.

15. The plan is (composed, comprised, constituted) of three parts.

16. The bill (will, would) provide more funding for airport security.

17. For more information, (call, contact) Sarah Jefferson at 555-5555.

18. He said that recent events had (convinced, persuaded) him to change his mind.

19. The first Harry Potter movie (debuted, had its debut) just before Christmas 2001.

20. She said the music was different (from, than) anything she had ever heard.

21. The (farther, further) the nation gets from the Florida election dispute, the more it seems to be forgotten.

22. This recipe has (fewer, less) ingredients than you might think.

23. Women were (forbidden, prohibited) from appearing in public without covering their heads.

24. They said they appreciated (him, his) helping out.

25. Flags around the country were flown at (half-mast, half-staff).

26. State legislators say they want to (hike, increase) property taxes again.

27. (Hopefully, Many Americans hope) that will be the last of the terrorist attacks.

28. Experts say (its, it's) not clear what the statement (implies, infers).

29. But (if, whether, whether or not) the dispute (lead, led) to the (death, murder) won't be decided until the trial next week.

30. For Bill and (I, me, myself), that's it for us here at Newscenter Nine.

31. None (has, have) come forward and confessed.

32. Not only has the Senate passed the measure, (but also so, but so) has the House.

33. (Currently, Presently), the play is (having its premiere, premiering) in Paris.

34. That's (what we're fighting for, the reason we're fighting).

35. (Before, Prior to) moving here, she lived in Montreal.

36. The missing Irish (Setter, setter) was found in a (dumpster, trash bin).

37. The rivers are (raising, rising) at flood speed.

38. The County Commission will hold (its, their) next meeting Wednesday night.

39. The couple's house was (burglarized, robbed) while they were on vacation.

40. He said it was (setting, sitting) on the table when he left the house.

41. The (African-American candidate, candidate) for mayor visited the Boys Club in the neighborhood Saturday.

42. Rassel said he wants to (precisely do, do precisely) that.

43. One of the suspects in the robbery (was, were) arrested at a mall later that day.

44. The inventor said it wasn't (suppose, supposed) to be used for that purpose.

45. The children watched their Rugrats movie, (which, that) featured a Kwanzaa celebration.

46. Terrorists (that, who) are captured may face military tribunals.

47. The secretary of the Navy said he would (use, utilize) ships already (under way, underway) to the area.

48. (Although, Though, While) the package didn't arrive on time, it still took less time than the previous one from this company.

49. The prize will be awarded to (whoever, whomever) is the 500th customer to walk through the door.

50. Peterman said he didn't know (who's, whose) fault it was.

B. Put the letter of the correctly written sentence in the space before the number.

_____ **1. a.** The garden club's next meeting will be Saturday. The topic will be winter gardening.
b. The garden club's next meeting will be Saturday, the topic will be winter gardening.

_____ **2. a.** Being an editing teacher, many people's grammar seems bad to her.
b. Being an editing teacher, she notices many people's bad grammar.

_____ **3. a.** The City Council voted to ban smoking in your own home if it offended a neighbor!
b. The City Council voted to ban smoking in your own home if it offended a neighbor.

_____ **4. a.** The Consumer Confidence Index climbed in December by 8.8 points, its biggest monthly increase in almost four years.
b. The Consumer Confidence Index climbed in December by 8.8 points. Its biggest monthly increase in almost four years.

_____ **5. a.** Tyson said that was a crime he'd long ago paid for.
b. Tyson said that was a crime for which he'd long ago paid.

_____ **6. a.** French actress, Arielle Dombasle, is married to one of France's leading philosophers Bernard-Henri Lévy.
b. French actress Arielle Dombasle is married to one of France's leading philosophers, Bernard-Henri Lévy.

_____7. **a.** Survivors include one brother, Paul Sasson of Denver, one sister, Emily Barton of Chicago, and two grandchildren.
b. Survivors include one brother, Paul Sasson of Denver; one sister, Emily Barton of Chicago; and two grandchildren.

_____8. **a.** The president said Friday that key objectives of his effort were met.
b. The president said Friday key objectives of his effort were met.

_____9. **a.** A student should check their work before handing it in.
b. Students should check their work before handing it in.

_____10. **a.** He said he used to find ethnic jokes funny but no more.
b. He said he use to find ethnic jokes funny, but no more.

Phrases, Clauses and Sentences

Name: _____

Class: _____

Date: _____

Short Answer

1. What do phrases, clauses and sentences have in common?

2. What's the difference between a phrase and a clause?

3. What's the difference between a clause and a sentence?

4. What are the two principal kinds of clauses?

5. What are the two kinds of dependent clauses?

6. What do the terms *restrictive* and *nonrestrictive* mean?

7. What are the four kinds of sentences classified by form?

8. Write a simple sentence.

9. Now, add a second thought to it in the form of an independent clause to make a compound sentence.

10. Next, go back to your original simple sentence and add a dependent clause to it to make a complex sentence.

11. Finally, combine your compound and complex sentences to make a single compound-complex one.

12. Write a complex sentence with a subordinate clause.

13. Now, write a complex sentence with a relative clause.

Phrases, Clauses and Sentences

Name: _____

Class: _____

Date: _____

Practice: Phrases, Clauses and Sentences

Phrases

In each of the following sentences, a phrase is underlined. Determine what kind of word it takes the place of, and in the blank in front of the number, put *SO* for subject or object, *V* for verb, *M* for modifier or *C* for connecting word.

_____ **1.** Jeffers admits, "To finish on time seems unlikely now."

_____ **2.** "No one is going to throw his elbows at me," the guard said.

_____ **3.** The new fire station will be built on the site of the old one.

_____ **4.** They were watching television when the storm hit.

_____ **5.** According to court documents, the company was having trouble as early as two years ago.

Clauses

In each of the following sentences, a clause is underlined. Determine whether it is an independent or dependent clause. In the blank in front of the number, put *I* if it's an independent clause. If it's a dependent clause, put *S* if it's subordinate or *R* if it's relative.

_____ **1.** The Vikings pulled out a victory in the final moments of the game.

_____ **2.** "It was fun," she said, "because Mr. Gillean made us laugh a lot."

_____ **3.** The tentative service area will include London and Whiteford townships, which had petitioned the board last year.

_____ **4.** Since that incident rocked the community, attitudes have changed.

_____ **5.** Cell phones are rapidly becoming an important tool for crooks, as they are for everyone else.

Restrictive vs. Nonrestrictive

A. Read each of the following sentences and determine whether the underlined word, phrase or clause is restrictive or nonrestrictive. Put *R* if it's restrictive, *N* if it's nonrestrictive.

_____**1.** Her husband, Ken, works as an insurance agent.

_____**2.** The airlines, which suffered major losses after Sept. 11, have asked the government for help.

_____**3.** The tree limbs that fell during the storm need to be hauled away.

_____**4.** When he was in school, he said, he always enjoyed math.

_____**5.** A NASA spacecraft that had been damaged in testing and repaired was sent into orbit today.

B. Use proper copy-editing symbols to fix punctuation in the following sentences according to whether the modifiers are restrictive or nonrestrictive. Do not rewrite the sentences. If the context is not clear enough to determine the author's intended meaning, write a query.

1. Former University of Missouri student, Gloria Julow Gillis, will be the featured artist in an exhibition next week at the Columbia Art League.

2. Phyllis Tewes, whose family now lives in Bloomington, Ind. said her son will always remain special to her.

3. From the corner, the third house that has a lawn jockey attacking a pink flamingo is mine.

4. Wilbur and Ann Bogdonovich announce the engagement of their daughter April to Mark Faber.

5. Margaret Mitchell's one novel "Gone With the Wind" has proved a favorite with readers.

6. Filmmaker, Woody Allen, is one of his favorites.

7. This latest poem your best I think is a good example of what I mean.

8. The building, across the street, is the library.

9. John as well as Henry says he will attend.

10. I don't however believe him.

Sentence Errors

A. Label each of the following *FR* for fragment, *S* for sentence, *CS* for comma splice, *FU* for fused or *R* for run-on.

_____ **1.** I'm not going out with her.

_____ **2.** No matter how often she asks.

_____ **3.** The computer works fine, so does the modem.

_____ **4.** Leonard Cohen's songs are dark and moody, but Bob Dylan's are usually more cheerful, but sometimes he can be as obscure as Cohen, but then again, he's more surrealistic, whereas Cohen is surrealistic, too, but mainly just plain weird, although sometimes he's funny, too, like Dylan but not usually.

_____ **5.** Because I want to.

_____ **6.** That's what I'm going to do I'm going to talk to him.

_____ **7.** Stephenson's. Home of great apple pie.

B. Rewrite the following sentences to make them parallel in construction.

1. First, read the introduction to each chapter, then you should complete the exercise.

2. Co-workers say the new boss is intelligent, friendly, and he inspires them.

Sentence Errors

A. Label each of the following [illegible] fragment [illegible] (Use [illegible] use I or X not cut [illegible]

___ 1. [illegible] outside [illegible]

___ 2. [illegible]

___ 3. [illegible] worked [illegible]

___ 4. [illegible] Cooper [illegible] is [illegible]

___ 5. Because I want [illegible]

___ 6. That's what I'm going to do [illegible] talk to him

___ 7. [illegible] Home [illegible] people

B. [illegible]

[illegible]

[illegible]

Phrases, Clauses and Sentences

Name: _____

Class: _____

Date: _____

Review: Phrases, Clauses and Sentences

Phrases

In each of the following sentences, a phrase is underlined. Determine what kind of word it takes the place of, and in the blank in front of the number, put *SO* for subject or object, *V* for verb, *M* for modifier or *C* for connecting word.

_____ **1.** In spite of the attack, she says she tries to remain positive.

_____ **2.** Recovered now from the accident, he says he feels lucky things have healed so well.

_____ **3.** Riding a stationary bike is his main exercise these days.

_____ **4.** To stop paying benefits now could cost many laid-off workers their homes.

_____ **5.** "We hope to attract some bids from minority contractors," Terwilliger said.

Clauses

In each of the following sentences, a clause is underlined. Determine whether it is an independent or dependent clause. In the blank in front of the number put *I* if it's an independent clause. If it's a dependent clause, put *S* if it's subordinate or *R* if it's relative.

_____ **1.** The software package is currently available only for Mac OS X and Linux, but the company says it hopes to have a Windows version out next month.

_____ **2.** "Whoever said this wouldn't work should come down here now," Brosnahan said.

_____ **3.** Although the weather was not ideal for soccer, the game proved one of the season's best for the Wizards.

_____ **4.** He said it was the strangest car that he had ever seen.

_____ **5.** The two were led away in handcuffs after the hearing ended.

Restrictive vs. Nonrestrictive

A. Read each of the following sentences and determine whether the underlined word, phrase or clause is restrictive or nonrestrictive. Put *R* if it's restrictive, *N* if it's nonrestrictive.

_____ **1.** Then there are the Afghan soldiers who have run out of food and supplies.

_____ **2.** "Yes, Virginia, there is a Santa Claus."

_____3. Last year, the company reported it had its highest earnings in the soft-drinks division.

_____4. That young singer—Celine Dion—has long since moved on to international stardom.

_____5. "Whoever they are will be found," the sheriff said.

B. Use proper copy-editing symbols to fix punctuation in the following sentences according to whether the modifiers are restrictive or nonrestrictive. Do not rewrite the sentences. If the context is not clear enough to determine the author's intended meaning, write a query.

1. His wife Susan was also there.

2. Stephen King's novel, "Cujo," sold well as usual for his books.

3. John McLaughlin has played guitar in many genres of music. This album by him for example is jazz.

4. John Horner who is a playwright will be there.

5. The ring, that his wife gave him when they married, has an inscription on the inside.

6. The program, that I saw last night, was excellent.

7. Shakespeare's well-known play, "The Merchant of Venice," is where we find the speech about "the quality of mercy."

8. The person who did that should be ashamed.

9. Don't drink the water unless you have a strong stomach.

10. There should be a comma according to what my teacher said before the word _too_ at the end of a sentence.

11. I'd like to, although, I don't think I can.

12. She, though disagreed.

Sentence Errors

A. Label each of the following _FR_ for fragment, _S_ for sentence, _CS_ for comma splice, _FU_ for fused or _R_ for run-on.

_____1. When the thunderstorm came, the sparse crowd ran up the steps to gather under the overhanging second deck.

_____2. Revenge!

_____ **3.** The statewide unemployment rate rose in December to 3.3 percent, up 1.1 percent from November's 2.2 percent, sparking fears in the capital that if the recession continues, not only will many families and individuals suffer but also that the state's tax revenues to fund programs like education will be endangered, and the state's initiative to force people on welfare to find work will also be put in jeopardy by the worsening economy, which could then be bad news for legislators come the fall elections when dissatisfaction over the job situation might be taken out on office holders.

_____ **4.** "I don't know how people afford to live there the housing costs are so high."

_____ **5.** The president signed the bill into law Wednesday, Congress passed it two weeks earlier.

B. Rewrite the following sentence to make it parallel in construction.

My favorite sports activities are playing soccer, Australian-rules football on television and to go to a baseball game.

Name: _____

Class: _____

Date: _____

Short Answer

1. What are the three cases of nouns and pronouns, and when do you use each?

2. Which case of nouns and pronouns is used as an adjective?

3. What's the difference between a common noun and a proper noun?

4. What's the difference between intensive and reflexive pronouns?

5. What's the difference between *that* and *who?*

6. What's the difference between *that* and *which?*

7. What's the difference between *who* and *whom, whoever* and *whomever?*

Subjects and Objects

Name: _____

Class: _____

Date: _____

Practice: Nouns

Common Nouns vs. Proper Nouns

A. Use proper copy-editing symbols to correct the following generic terms and brand names.

1. aqualung

2. band-aid

3. jeep

4. kitty litter

5. Naugahyde

6. realtor

7. Scotch tape

8. styrofoam

9. velcro

10. Xerox

B. Use proper copy-editing symbols to correct the capitalization of the following names according to the rules for animals, foods and plants.

1. lily of the valley

2. German Shepherd

3. french fries

4. basset hound

5. Bavarian Cream

6. Italian Bread

7. Waldorf Salad

8. irish setter

Forming Singulars and Plurals of Nouns

Write the plural for each of the following nouns.

1. attorney general

2. B

3. datum

4. Dolly

5. hero

6. jelly

7. knife

8. medium

9. ox

10. phenomenon

11. tornado

12. try

Forming Possessives of Nouns

A. Circle the correct answers.

1. The preacher ended his prayer with "in (Jesuses, Jesus', Jesus's) name, amen."

2. Is this where the (Smith's, Smiths, Smiths') live?

3. Is this the (Smith's, Smiths, Smiths') house?

4. This pizza belongs to the (Jones', Jones, Joneses', Joneses).

5. This pizza is the (Jones', Jones, Joneses', Joneses).

6. The (attorney generals', attorney general's) decision is expected next month.

7. The cabin belongs to the (sons-in-law, son-in-laws) jointly.

8. The two (mother-in-laws', mothers-in-law's) beliefs were at odds.

9. (Bill, Bill's) and Henry's grades left something to be desired.

B. Circle the correct phrase in each group.

1. baker's dozen, bakers' dozen

2. baker's yeast, bakers' yeast

3. children's theater, childrens theater

4. nurses aide, nurse's aide, nurses' aide

Practice: Pronouns

Pronoun Agreement

Circle the correct answers in the following sentences for correct pronoun-antecedent agreement and for clear pronoun reference.

1. A reporter should check (his, his or her, their, there, they're) copy.

2. The City Council said (it, they) would consider the sewer issue at tonight's public hearing.

3. The committee will hold (its, it's, their, there, they're) next meeting Monday.

4. The Detroit Tigers will play (its, it's, their, there, they're) next game at home.

5. Everyone has had (his, his or her, their) ego bruised at some time or other.

6. No one can accomplish anything unless (he tries, he or she tries, they try).

7. As she stood before the audience at the assembly, she froze for a moment as she looked at (their faces, its faces, the faces).

8. After the game, the team went to (its, it's, their, there, they're) homes.

9. The committee members are split in (its, it's, their, there, they're) political leanings.

10. The board voted for the ban under the gun of federal regulators who threatened to cut funding if (it, they) didn't.

Clear Pronoun Reference

Rewrite the following sentences as necessary to correct unclear pronoun reference.

1. It's not known whether his brother and his wife were on the plane.

2. The jury had to consider their own conscience as well as the law.

3. Before she recommended the student, Young read his résumé.

Pronoun Cases

Circle the correct answers.

1. Between you and (I, me), this looks easier than I thought.

2. Valerie was mistaken to be (her, she). And they mistook (her, she) to be (her, she).

3. (Us, We) journalism students have it bad but not so bad as (them, they).

4. Is Terry's husband older than (her, she)?

5. Neither (he, him) nor (her, she) could make it.

6. They said they had thought it was (her, she) and (I, me) who went to the costume party

    as the "Love Boat."

7. She said (it's, its) not (it's, its) fault.

8. (Who's, Whose) book is this? (Who's, Whose) going to claim it?

Relative Pronouns

Circle the correct answers.

1. The cannon belongs to the Mayflower Hotel, (that, which, who, whom) is one of the or-

    ganizers of the rally.

2. It's a mistake to give your credit card number to (whoever, whomever) asks for it.

3. (Who, Whom) did the City Council appoint to the post?

4. Nobody seems to know (who, whom) to call for information.

5. The deputies (that, which, who, whom) the sheriff chastised refused to comment.

6. The victim, (that, which, who, whom) was identified as Will Beason, was a drifter.

7. Did she say (who, whom) we would be reading in this course?

8. (Whoever, Whomever) is going should line up here.

9. (Who, Whom) was it (that, which, who, whom) played bass in The Doors?

10. The animals (that, which, who, whom) need protecting most are put on the list.

Pronouns Ending in Self or Selves

Circle the correct answers.

1. For Joann and (I, me, myself), good night.

2. Give the information to either Steve or (I, me).

3. It's (I, me, myself)!

4. Include a picture of (you, yourself).

Verbal Nouns

Circle the correct answers.

1. We enjoyed (him, his) playing soccer.

2. The wrestler weighs 450 pounds. Can you imagine (him, his) falling on (you, yourself)?

8. Whoever (Whomever) is going should line up here.

9. [illegible] Who (Whom) [illegible] that [illegible] friend who (whom) [illegible]

10. The athletes [illegible] who (whom) [illegible] most [illegible] list.

Exercise [illegible] for Self-[illegible]

Circle the [illegible]

1. [illegible] and [illegible] (myself) [illegible]

2. Give the information to either [illegible] or (I/me).

3. [illegible]

4. [illegible]

Name [illegible]

[illegible]

1. [illegible]

2. [illegible]

Subjects and Objects

Name: _____

Class: _____

Date: _____

Review: Nouns

Common Nouns vs. Proper Nouns

A. Use proper copy-editing symbols to correct the following generic terms and brand names.

1. Astroturf

2. dumpster

3. jello

4. laundromat

5. novocain

6. rollerblades

7. seeing-eye dog

8. Windbreaker

9. ziplock bag

B. Use proper copy-editing symbols to correct the capitalization of the following names according to the rules for animals, foods and plants.

1. Boston cream pie

2. dutch elm

3. Red Delicious Apple

4. Russian dressing

5. swiss cheese

6. granny Smith apple

7. manhattan cocktail

8. Graham crackers

Forming Singulars and Plurals of Nouns

Write the plural of each noun.

1. bacterium

2. belly

3. child

4. criterium

5. F

6. graffito

7. Jimmy

8. mother-in-law

9. potato

10. self

11. volcano

Forming Possessives of Nouns

A. Circle the correct answers.

1. The (attorney generals, attorneys general) of most of the states met over the summer.

2. (Fred's and Edie's, Fred and Edie's) car was blue.

3. The (Wilsons, Wilsons', Wilson's) are coming over for dinner tonight.

4. Carla Fredericks is on her way to visit the rest of the (Fredericks, Frederickses, Fredericks', Frederickses').

5. The same house used to belong to the (Grants, Grants', Grantses').

B. Circle the correct phrase in each group.

1. boatmans holiday, boatman's holiday

2. teacher's college, teachers' college, teachers college

3. women's college, womens' college, womens college

4. writer's guide, writers' guide, writers guide

Review: Pronouns

Pronoun Agreement

Circle the correct answers.

1. All have done (his, their) part.

2. Everyone deserves to get (his, her, his or her, their) wish.

3. Either he or they are going to sing (his, their) song next.

4. Either they or he is going to sing (his, their) song next.

5. Neither Bill nor Shirley would do (her, his, his or her, their) part.

6. Each of the birds in the flock has (his, her, its, their) own personality.

7. The board will decide the issue at (its, their) next meeting.

8. None of the men worked out as well as the committee hoped (he, he or she, they) would.

Clear Pronoun Reference

Rewrite the following sentences as necessary to correct unclear pronoun references.

1. It's raining outside.

2. Before he visited the site, he said, Diaz had no idea how big it was.

3. When Wilson and Pinter were speaking, he asked him whether he could handle the project.

Pronoun Cases

Circle the correct answers.

1. It's (I, me)!

2. They believed John to be (I, me, myself).

3. You and (I, me, myself) have much in common.

4. Would you hand these to (he, him) and (her, she)?

5. We hope Bill and (her, herself, she) will visit soon.

6. They picked (he, him, himself) to win the race.

7. Carol was assumed to be (her, she) in the window—wasn't it (her, she)?

8. Is this (your's, yours)?

9. That car is (their's, theirs).

10. The air is (everybodies', everybody's, everybodys).

Relative Pronouns

Circle the correct answers.

1. To (who, whom) are you talking?

2. Collect the money from (whoever, whomever) will pay it.

3. (Whoever, Whomever) would have thought the Kansas City Wizards would win the MLS Cup in 2000?

4. (Who, Whom) are you going to get to play the organ this week at church?

5. By (who, whom) was this painted?

6. The impersonator can imitate (whoever, whomever) you want him to be.

7. The fish (that, which, who, whom) got away may be the one (that, which, who, whom) old-timers call "Big Wally."

8. The books (that, which) interest me the most are classics.

9. Bill Seraphim, the hospital president, told the board Monday that Wyandotte Health Services, (that, which, who, whom) is leasing the hospital, has plans to solve the space shortage.

10. The jetliner (that, which) crashed in the mountains near Grand Junction, Colo., was headed for Los Angeles. The plane, (that, which) was carrying 83 passengers, had radioed it was having engine trouble.

Pronouns Ending in **Self** *or* **Selves**

Circle the correct answers.

1. Hand it to him or (I, me, myself).

2. My husband and (I, me, myself) visited the exhibit this past weekend.

3. I did it to save (me, myself) time.

4. To save (me, myself) money, I would have done something else.

Verbal Nouns

Circle the correct answers.

1. And that was the end of (him, his) barking.

2. They said they couldn't stand the (customers, customers') constant complaints.

Subject-Verb Agreement

Name: _____

Class: _____

Date: _____

Practice: Subject-Verb Agreement

Conjunctions

Circle the correct answers.

1. Alan and Henry (are, is) going.

2. Alan, as well as Henry, (are, is) going.

3. Pork and beans (are, is) a favorite Western dish.

4. Peas and carrots (are, is) not his favorite vegetable dish.

5. Mashed potatoes and gravy (are, is) a favorite dish with steak.

6. He, as well as they, (know, knows) the hidden message.

Collective Nouns

For each of the following words, put *S* in front of the word if it is *normally* singular, *P* if it is *normally* plural or *SP* if it can go either way in roughly equal proportions depending on the phrase in which it appears.

_____ 1. association   _____ 7. faculty   _____ 13. panel

_____ 2. commission   _____ 8. few   _____ 14. percent

_____ 3. committee   _____ 9. jury   _____ 15. remainder

_____ 4. corporation   _____ 10. little   _____ 16. several

_____ 5. council   _____ 11. most   _____ 17. total

_____ 6. couple   _____ 12. number

Uncountable Nouns

For each of the following, put *S* in front of the word if it is always singular, *P* if it is always plural or *SP* if it can be either one depending on the context.

_____ 1. athletics   _____ 4. measles   _____ 7. pliers

_____ 2. ethics   _____ 5. mumps   _____ 8. politics

_____ 3. mathematics   _____ 6. news   _____ 9. scissors

Other Confusing Nouns

For each of the following, put *S* in front of the word if it is always singular, *P* if it is always plural or *SP* if it can be either one depending on the context.

_____ 1. alumni

_____ 2. bacteria

_____ 3. criteria

_____ 4. data

_____ 5. media

_____ 6. oxen

_____ 7. phenomenon

Indefinite Pronouns

For each of the following, put *S* in front of the word if it is always singular, *P* if it is always plural or *SP* if it can be either one depending on the context.

_____ 1. all

_____ 2. anybody

_____ 3. each

_____ 4. either

_____ 5. everyone

_____ 6. neither

_____ 7. no one

_____ 8. nothing

_____ 9. one

_____ 10. some

_____ 11. what

Intervening Nouns and Pronouns

Circle the correct answers.

1. No one but they (know, knows) the answer.

2. Only one of the 12 professors (seem, seems) interesting.

3. She said she hopes for a cure for AIDS as a team of testers (search, searches).

4. The state of Missouri is one of those that (has, have) filed legal opposition to Clark's ruling.

5. Only one of the 20 (has, have) agreed.

6. Each of them (are, is) going by car.

7. Each (are, is) going by car.

8. They (are, is) each going by car.

9. Kelly is one of the girls who (was, were) nominated.

Subject and Predicate Nominative in Disagreement

Circle the correct answers.

1. The panel (are, is) Betty, Bill and Joan.

2. Betty, Bill and Joan (are, is) the panel.

3. The committee (are, is) Scotty, Brian and Phil.

Inverted Order

Circle the correct answers.

1. Out of the book (come, comes) three ideas.

2. Here (come, comes) the Wilsons!

3. (There's, There are) three "nevers" in comedy.

4. (Here are, Here's) two rules you shouldn't forget.

5. (There are, There's) a few of them now.

6. There (aren't, isn't) enough data.

7. (Here are, Here's) a few of the books you requested.

8. What he ordered (was, were) computer disks.

Subject-Verb Agreement

Name: _____

Class: _____

Date: _____

Review: Subject-Verb Agreement

Circle the correct answers.

1. The Sufi sage said the evils of the world (are, is) what God permits to thicken the plot.

2. The jury (disagree, disagrees) on a verdict.

3. The media (was, were) there to cover the accident before the ambulance arrived.

4. The committee (was, were) split over the amendment.

5. Physicists now think of atomic particles as something that (pop, pops) in and out of existence according to chance.

6. The radio said 1 to 3 inches of snow (are, is) possible.

7. One-third of the students (are, is) from out of state.

8. About 50 percent of the project (are, is) unfinished.

9. The committee (are, is) agreed.

10. The committee (are, is) disagreed.

11. Mumps (are, is) seldom fatal.

12. The number of people (are, is) small.

13. A total of 30 (are, is) going.

14. None of the local dealers (was, were) there.

15. None of them (agree, agrees) about what should be done.

16. A number of researchers (was, were) shocked by the report.

Name: _____

Class: _____

Date: _____

Short Answer

1. What's the difference between a *transitive* verb and an *intransitive* verb?

2. What are the two kinds of intransitive verbs?

3. List the principal parts of the verb *to lie*.

4. Conjugate the verb *to raise* in all six tenses. Label the tenses.

5. Conjugate the verb *to write* in third-person singular for all six progressive forms. Label each form.

6. Define passive voice, and list its three characteristics.

7. List the names of the four moods of a verb, and tell how each is used.

8. Conjugate the verb *to sing* in all its imperative-mood forms.

9. get

10. hang (execute)

11. hang (suspend)

12. lay

13. lie (recline)

14. pay

15. plead

16. prove

17. raise

18. rise

19. set

20. sit

21. swear

22. swim

Sequence of Tenses

Circle the correct answers.

1. She said she (is, was) smarter than that now.

2. Professor Ian Hathaway said the moon (is, was) a satellite.

3. "I think he's (prejudice, prejudiced)," she said.

4. These parts aren't fitting together as they're (suppose, supposed) to do.

Voice

Put a check in front of each passive-voice sentence.

_____ **1.** The story was edited by the copy desk.

_____ **2.** The copy desk has edited the story.

_____ **3.** The story was edited.

_____ **4.** Was this story edited?

_____ **5.** Has anyone edited this story?

_____ **6.** The medicine has been proved to be effective.

_____ **7.** The medicine is proven effective.

_____ **8.** He burned the toast.

_____ **9.** The toast was burned.

_____ **10.** The toast was burnt.

_____ **11.** I was lost.

_____ **12.** Too many assignments were due at once.

_____ **13.** The president was hardly elected in a landslide.

_____**14.** The professor was acting pretty strangely.

_____**15.** The commissioner was arrested for tax evasion.

_____**16.** Police said the man was shot several times in the chest.

Mood

Circle the correct answers.

1. I wouldn't if I (was, were) you.

2. She moved that the resolution (be, is) approved.

3. He demanded that the committee (decide, decides) now.

4. If he (sing, sings), will you attend?

5. If she (was, were) coming, she'd be here by now.

6. He plays piano as though he (was, were) a professional.

7. When someone sneezes, we say "God (bless, blesses) you."

8. If she (be, is) guilty, she should go to prison.

9. I wish I (was, were) through with this assignment.

10. If I hurt your feelings, I (am, be) sorry.

11. He said he could do the job better if he (had, has, have) better tools.

12. If this (be, is) what I think it (be, is), then it (be, is) an important finding.

13. His mom insisted that he (stay, stays) home and (help, helps) with the dishes.

14. I prefer that you (go, goes).

15. They recommended he (take, takes) more classes in English.

Nouns Used as Verbs

Circle the correct answers.

1. For more information about (holding, hosting) a Tupperware party, (call, contact) Belinda Hamilton at 555-1212.

2. The movie, (aimed, targeted) at a younger audience, (has its premiere, premieres) Thursday.

3. William Least Heat-Moon (authored, wrote) the popular "Blue Highways."

4. The director said she needs to (make, process) a few script changes before the production is ready to (debut, have its debut).

5. None of our neighbors (flies, jets) to the Bahamas for the weekend!

6. He read a book to learn how to (parent, raise) his daughter better.

7. The English teacher said children need more practice (languaging on paper, writing).

8. We need someone strong to (chairman, lead) the committee.

3. The director said she [illegible] (produce, process) a few script changes [illegible] the premiere [illegible] (debut)

4. [illegible] of the neighbors [illegible] to the Bahamas for the weekend.

5. [illegible] a book [illegible] (parent, raise) his [illegible] characters.

[illegible]

8. [illegible] strong [illegible] and the [illegible]

Verbs

Review: Verbs

Regular Verbs vs. Irregular Verbs

Circle the correct answers.

1. I think I'll go (lay, lie) down.

2. For several days, he just (lay, laid, lied) around, doing nothing.

3. (Sit, Set) the bag of cement down over there.

4. Don't (sit, set) down over there until the concrete in the walk has had a chance to

   (set, sit).

5. The lake level is (raising, rising) higher than it has in the past.

6. (Raise, Rise) up for a minute, will you?

7. Has your new job (brought, brung) you any happiness?

8. I had (got, gotten) up early that morning.

9. They (hanged, hung) the condemned man at midnight.

10. When my back has been hurting, sometimes I've (laid, lain, lied) down on the floor at

    home.

11. I had just (sat, satted, set, setted) down when the phone rang.

12. When she came home from work, she found that her husband had (hanged, hung) all the

    pictures in their new home.

13. The defendant (pleaded, pled) guilty.

14. A 3-year-old Mayfield child (drown, drowned, drowneded) Wednesday in a pond behind

    her home. A neighbor saw her fall in and (dived, dove) in after her but was too late.

15. That was the year "Saturday Night Live" was first (broadcast, broadcasted).

16. When they came home from visiting their grandparents over Christmas, they found their water pipes had frozen and (burst, bust, bursted, busted).

17. When's the next time we get (paid, payed)?

18. I know I (lay, laid, layed) those keys down somewhere!

19. One thing (lead, led) to another.

Sequence of Tenses

Circle the correct answers.

1. She said she (can't, couldn't) help as much as she'd like.

2. He said that before coming to Washington, he (had worked, worked) in New York.

3. Hixson said she (is, was) pleased with the way everything (has, had) come together.

4. He (use, used) to jog but gave it up.

Voice

Put a check beside each sentence with a passive-voice verb.

_____**1.** The police were searching for more evidence.

_____**2.** The evidence was gathered over the weekend.

_____**3.** The exam was given promptly at noon.

_____**4.** The man shot the mayor.

_____**5.** The bills were due.

_____**6.** It was hard for him to see in the dark room.

_____**7.** The noise was deafening.

_____**8.** The election was held in secret.

_____**9.** The sun was shining.

_____**10.** Damage to the house and its contents was estimated by the Fire Department to be about $200,000.

_____**11.** Police said no one was seen leaving the building.

_____**12.** The fire investigator said no evidence of arson was found.

_____**13.** The downtown First National Bank was robbed this morning of about $25,000 by a man wearing a Halloween mask of President George W. Bush.

_____**14.** Sam Smothers, 28, of Ashland was killed when the car he was driving was struck by a pickup heading north on U.S. 63.

_____**15.** No charges have been filed.

_____**16.** A good time was had by all.

_____**17.** All her spare time is devoted to the game.

Mood

Circle the correct answers.

1. I might do it if I (was, were) asked.

2. They ask only that she (return, returns) the merchandise.

3. I (am, be) happy.

4. It's necessary that I (am, be) left alone.

5. If I (was, were) going to go, I'd have dressed by now.

6. If he (be, is) guilty, he should hang.

7. If this (be, is) heaven, (I'll, I should, I would) take hell.

8. If he (was, were) any taller, we'd have to raise the ceiling.

9. If he (edit, edits) this by tomorrow, (will, would) you reconsider lowering his grade?

10. I demand that she (stay, stays).

11. I insist that he (go, goes).

12. I doubt that he (know, knows) right from wrong.

13. I suppose that you (are, be) right.

14. Lest he forget, I (shall, should) remind him.

15. Be that as it (may, might), she (can, could) do as she (like, likes).

16. First, read the introduction to each chapter, then (complete, you should complete) the exercise.

17. If the new policy (be, is) not overturned by the courts, companies (will, would) be required to have programs in place by December.

Nouns Used as Verbs

Circle the correct answers.

1. There seemed to be a big (disconnect, disconnection) between the media and the

   American public over the scandal.

2. The people of the village (gave me, gifted me with) this necklace.

3. Let's (dialogue, talk) next week and (ink, sign) a contract.

4. The Institute for Objectivist Studies (has its headquarters, is headquartered) in

   Poughkeepsie, N.Y.

5. They'll take a (victory, win) wherever they can find one.

Name: _____

Class: _____

Date: _____

Short Answer

1. What characteristics do adjectives and adverbs share?

2. Name the three degrees of comparison, and explain how to form them—first for adjectives, then for adverbs.

3. Define and give the two characteristics of coordinate adjectives.

4. How should coordinate adjectives be punctuated?

5. What common kinds of adjectives are we not considering coordinate adjectives?

6. What is a compound modifier?

7. In general, how should compound modifiers be punctuated when they precede the word they modify? What are the common exceptions?

8. Which words are considered articles? What part of speech are they?

9. What are three things that adverbs tend to tell us?

10. What is a sentence adverb? What sentence adverb is most likely to get you into trouble?

11. Should adverbs ever come between the parts of a verb phrase? If so, when and when not?

12. We're calling interjections modifiers because they often resemble what?

13. Which two kinds of verbals are often used as modifiers?

14. How can you tell the difference between a participle used in forming a passive-voice verb and a participle used as a predicate adjective?

15. What is a dangling participle? A nominative absolute?

Modifiers

Name: _____

Class: _____

Date: _____

Practice: Modifiers

Comparative Forms of Adjectives and Adverbs

A. List the three degrees of comparison for each of these adjectives.

1. bad

2. beautiful

3. big

4. dark

5. easy

6. famous

7. far

8. fast

9. good

10. little

11. many

12. old

B. List the three degrees of comparison for each of these adverbs.

1. badly

2. carefully

3. fast

4. likely

5. quickly

6. soon

7. well

Adjectives vs. Adverbs

Circle the correct answers.

1. This brew goes down (more smoothly, smoother) than that one.

2. The car was traveling (quick, quickly).

3. I finished (more slowly, slower) than most.

4. Flowers smell (sweet, sweetly) this time of year.

5. I feel (bad, badly) about that.

6. The car ran (good, well) after the tuneup.

7. The new father looked (proud, proudly) as he left the hospital.

8. She hit her brakes (more quickly, quicker) than the other driver.

9. We drove (real, really) (slow, slowly) through the fog.

10. The parking meters were checked (regular, regularly).

Coordinate Adjectives vs. Compound Modifiers

Use proper copy-editing symbols to insert commas or hyphens where needed in the following sentences.

1. The short pudgy man wearing a gardenia is I.

2. The part time worker is well liked.

3. The tall thin gentleman is my uncle.

4. The spotted black dog bit the happy looking man

5. The partially completed work has not been touched in years.

6. He's old fashioned but well liked.

7. The 36 year old man moved here four years ago.

8. Norton said he favored a gasoline tax increase to fund the $100 million project.

9. He was given a five to 10 year prison sentence.

10. She remembers it as a dark terrible night.

Articles

Circle the correct answers.

1. The higher education commissioner finds herself in (a, an) unique situation.

2. This is (a, an) historical occasion.

3. He holds (a, an) honorary doctorate from Tulane University.

Misplaced Modifiers

Rewrite the following sentences as needed to fix awkward modifier placement and to clarify meaning. If a sentence could have more than one meaning, pick the more probable, and rewrite accordingly. Also, query intent where you think it necessary.

1. Hanging from the cave ceiling, he saw thousands of bats.

2. However, it hasn't happened yet.

3. Phil Barnsworth said he wants to be "the jobs mayor" Friday.

4. The computer having gone down, the paper was late.

5. The award was developed after Robert Kennedy was assassinated by a group of journalists he traveled with during his presidential campaign in 1968.

6. Johnson only has one of the rare baseball cards.

7. I just want to quickly end this dispute.

8. After winning the race, a drug test stripped away his gold medal.

9. As a psychologist, a lot of our viewers may wonder what your connection is to sports.

10. Cleaned and crushed, distributors send the cans to aluminum recycling plants.

Modifiers

Review: Modifiers

Comparative Forms of Adjectives and Adverbs

Circle the correct answers.

1. He is the (older, oldest) of the three editors and has one of the more (unique, unusual) book collections I've ever seen.

2. Which of these two cars do you think is (better, best)?

3. She is the (younger, youngest) of the two sisters.

4. The winning driver was faster (than anyone, than anyone else) in the race.

5. More (important, importantly), this brand of computer costs less.

6. (Almost, Most) all of them are ready.

7. He said he (has smoked only once, hasn't smoked but once).

8. He was the (taller, tallest) of all the players on the basketball team.

9. Because of the smoke, you (can, can't) hardly see the mountains some days.

10. That (doesn't hardly ever happen, hardly ever happens).

11. The new professor we've hired has more years in the field than (anyone, anyone else) on the faculty.

12. Which of these two cars do you think is (best, better)?

Adjectives vs. Adverbs

Circle the correct answers.

1. At that question, Jimenez waxed (philosophical, philosophically).

2. I don't feel (good, well) today.

3. He did (good, well) on the final exam.

4. The new typesetter is working (real, really) (good, well).

5. He kicked the ball past the goalie (perfect, perfectly).

6. When the monk rang the bell, it sounded out (loud, loudly).

7. It looked to the coach that he was playing too (cautious, cautiously) for that field position.

8. The music sounded (loud, loudly) even though it was coming from the next building.

9. The pickles taste rather (sour, sourly).

10. She's performing rather (weak, weakly) in that role.

11. Turn the dial (slow, slowly), or you'll go right past the station.

12. (First, Firstly), let's consider our options.

13. I'm going to start having to eat (in a healthier way, more healthy).

14. Write it (correctly, right).

Coordinate Adjectives vs. Compound Modifiers

Use proper copy-editing symbols to insert commas or hyphens where needed in the following sentences.

1. The story about the old yellow dog is a sad one.

2. She is a part time worker. He works part time.

3. The 6 month old baby drowned Wednesday.

4. Although the short term problems of the drought could be corrected with a few inches of rain, the extension agent said long term problems would be more serious.

5. More than 40 people attended the third graders' play.

6. Small business incomes declined 3 percent in March.

7. The three planks were each 6 foot long boards.

8. She is a well respected poet, translator and editor.

9. The Saturday afternoon football game was played under a light blue sky.

10. The suspect in the child sex abuse case was originally arrested on a charge of armed criminal action.

11. The real estate agent decided she should get a blood pressure check.

12. The game's most valuable player spent the summer working in a walk in storage facility.

Articles

Circle the correct answers.

1. (Allott, A lot, Alot) of people would agree.

2. The alarm rang just (a while, awhile) ago.

3. It's (another, a whole nother) world out there!

Misplaced Modifiers

Rewrite the following sentences as needed to fix awkward modifier placements and to clarify meaning. Query intent if you think it necessary.

1. Going back for the fly ball, the sun got in his eyes.

2. The clock has been consistently gaining time.

3. To get ahead in the music business, the audience must be kept in mind. And they must enjoy your playing.

4. Seeing them again, it was as though it were 20 years ago.

5. She wants to not be disturbed.

6. Knowing that a dog won't eat what he can't smell, which dog food would you buy?

7. Two men—one carrying a bomb and the other an officer of the New Jewish Defense League—were arrested on charges of plotting to bomb an Arab tourist office.

8. People who work slowly adjust to the grind.

9. Burning on the ground, Myers saw the plane in the field.

10. From her point of view, it didn't make sense to Davis.

Connecting Words

Name: _____

Class: _____

Date: _____

Short Answer

1. What's an easy way to recognize most prepositions?

2. What things do prepositions tell us?

3. What do prepositions connect?

4. Prepositional phrases are used in place of what parts of speech?

5. What should you do if you find a sentence (not in a quotation) ending in a preposition?

6. What are the differences between coordinate conjunctions and subordinate conjunctions?

7. What are the differences between conjunctions and conjunctive adverbs?

8. What's the difference between a conjunction and a relative pronoun?

CHAPTER 7
Connecting Words

Name: _____

Class: _____

Date: _____

Connecting Words

A. Circle the correct answers.

1. The issue (centers around, centers on) the vice president's image.

2. (Prior to, Before) the operation, she was in constant pain.

3. Neither the alumni (or, nor) the students seem to favor the proposal.

4. His vase was different (from, than) the one at the museum; compared (to, with) his, the museum's looked plain.

5. The tests found the dog was free (from, of) disease.

6. She was wearing a dress identical (to, with) mine!

7. Police investigated the business (in which he was involved, which he was involved in) for mob connections.

8. This exercise is (to, too, two) easy.

9. He thought the shirt wasn't made (as, so) well as the ones he buys through the mail.

10. I don't know (if, whether, whether or not) I want to go.

11. (While, Although) we disagreed at the time with what he said, we later decided he had made some good points.

12. (Among, Between) the three of us, we can probably put together a proposal that will compare favorably (to, with) theirs.

13. (Among, Between) the two of us, we should try to help (each other, one another).

14. She was convicted (of, with) soliciting.

15. Not only he (also, but also, in addition) she agreed.

B. Choose the correct verb, depending on the connective following it, in the following two sentences.

1. He was (convinced, persuaded) that he should try to (convince, persuade) others to go

   to the seminar.

2. The administration said they were (forbidden, prohibited) from protesting.

C. Put a check in front of the grammatically preferable wording.

_____ He's the boy I'd like to give my baseball glove to.

_____ He's the boy to whom I'd like to give my baseball glove.

D. Put a check in front of the grammatically preferable headline.

_____ City to look
       into corruption charges

_____ City to look into
       corruption charges

E. Put a check in front of the correctly punctuated sentence.

_____ He thought this exercise the hardest because there were so many unrelated points to
       remember.

_____ He thought this exercise the hardest, because there were so many unrelated points to
       remember.

Usage

Practice: Usage

Circle the correct answers.

1. I want to watch that new show (that, which) gets (under way, underway) on (television, TV) tonight.

2. (Who, Whom) do you know at the United Nations (that, who) drinks Scotch (whiskey, whisky)?

3. About 300 (people, persons) showed up.

4. We enjoyed the (trek, trip) to the convention.

5. A verbal report (is an oral one, is a written one, may be oral or written).

6. At the air show, the group passed out a (flier, flyer) about a famous squadron of (fliers, flyers).

7. She had (blond, blonde) hair for (a while, awhile) until she became (convinced, persuaded) of the beauty of her natural color.

8. The department has $4 million in its budget this year, compared (to, with) $4.2 million last year, yet the need for its services among county (citizens, residents) is no different (from, than) what it was last year.

9. The 19-year-old (boy, man) (collided with, hit) a parked car when the gear jumped into reverse and his truck hurtled (backward, backwards).

10. She said that didn't (faze, phase) her.

11. Do you have a (couple, couple of) minutes?

12. A female graduate of a college is an (alumnus, alumna, alumnae, alumni).

13. He had just (laid, lay, layed, lain) down when the phone (rang, rung).

14. The Lugnuts are a minor-league baseball team in Lansing, the state (capital, Capitol).

15. A prisoner who is released early is out on (parole, probation); a person who is sentenced but not sent to jail is out on (parole, probation).

16. What's your (alibi, excuse) for missing the test?

17. Would you (lend, loan) me your home computer to write my term paper?

18. Why don't villains in soap operas ever get their just (deserts, desserts)?

19. That price represents a real (saving, savings)!

20. The report said 1,200 (troupes, troops, soldiers) died.

21. The farm bill was (adopted, approved, passed) by the Kansas Legislature.

22. Yesterday, I was so tired I (laid, lay, layed, lain) down on my couch and went to sleep.

23. To (assure, ensure, insure) we don't take too big a loss, we will (assure, ensure, insure) the shipment, I (assure, ensure, insure) you.

24. Fifty states (compose, comprise, constitute) the United States. Each state (comprises, is comprised of) many counties.

25. A speaker or writer (implies, infers); a listener or reader (implies, infers).

26. (Hopefully, I hope) it won't snow over Thanksgiving break.

27. Students were (forbidden, prohibited) to smoke in the building.

28. The spokesman said the government (anticipates, expects) enemy troop movements.

29. They decided to (flaunt, flout) the law by (flaunting, flouting) their armbands.

30. We'd better (marshal, marshall, martial) our arguments before we go into that meeting.

31. Janet was (poring, pouring) over a book when I arrived.

32. First, you (flounder, founder), then you (flounder, founder).

33. The New Zealanders (gibed, jibed) at the Australians because the protective skirt around their ship's hull didn't (gibe, jibe) with the sailors' idea of manliness.

34. The flags at City Hall were lowered to (half-staff, half-mast), and the ceremony was (underway, under way).

35. He was (amused, bemused, confused) by his friend's dry wit and smiled slightly.

36. A person who isn't married is (celibate, chaste); that doesn't mean, however, the person is (celibate, chaste).

37. The (enormity, enormousness) of the Nazi crimes cannot be forgiven.

38. Springfield is considering a new (sewage, sewerage) system to handle its (sewage, sewerage) problems.

39. If you'll come (and, to) cook, I'll try (and, to) eat it.

40. He is as (callous, callus) as the (callouses, calluses) on his hands.

41. Put the ship and the (naval, navel) document over the (mantel, mantle).

42. I'm (loath, loathe) to say it, but I (loath, loathe) that kind of music.

43. The smell from the (grill, grille) where they were cooking (hoards, hordes) of fish made me (nauseated, nauseous).

44. The workers let the (cement, concrete) walkway (set, sit) overnight.

45. The (affect, effect) was (masterful, masterly).

46. She (elicited, illicited) the details of the (elicit, illicit) dealings from the (eminent, immanent, imminent) author.

Usage

Name: _____

Class: _____

Date: _____

Review: Usage

Circle the correct answers.

1. He had just (laid, lain, lay, layed) down when someone kicked in his door and entered his house.

2. A tanker spill could affect all (citizens, residents) within a radius of several miles.

3. (A lot, Alot, Allot) of people showed up.

4. To talk with someone (farther, further) about this, you're going to have to travel a few miles (farther, further) to the (gas, gasoline) station where the police are waiting.

5. The president's (aid, aide) said he had not been told otherwise.

6. What will the (affect, effect) be? How will this (affect, effect) us?

7. (Whose, Who's) book is this?

8. (Set, Sit) the box down over here, please.

9. Her friends will (hold, host) the party to raise money for a campaign to (hike, increase) the social services budget.

10. Let's discuss this (among, between) the three of us.

11. Joan was feeling (eager, anxious) and was (eager, anxious) to get help from a psychotherapist.

12. (Irregardless, Regardless) of what the officer says, I'm innocent.

13. For the (last, latest, past) 10 years, she said, she's been working on her magnum opus.

14. (Prior to, Before) coming here, I worked in Colorado.

15. (As, Like) I was saying, it's been a long time.

16. The desert was (continual, continuous) as far as the eye could see.

17. She thought his manner (aggravating, annoying, irritating).

18. The figures look different (from, than) last year's.

19. I was (reluctant, reticent) to say it, but I was (reluctant, reticent) to go to the rally

    (because, since, due to the fact that) I didn't know anyone.

20. Remember, (choose, chose) and (loose, lose) rhyme.

21. The court ordered that the students be (bused, bussed).

22. For a good (back yard, backyard) (barbecue, barbeque, Bar-B-Q), the first thing you

    need is a (back yard, backyard).

23. (Every day, Everyday), (every one, everyone) should try hard.

24. The (premier, premiere) is the (premier, premiere) head of state in Europe.

25. He's not (as, so) smart as he thinks.

26. He didn't say (if, whether, whether or not) there would be a quiz today.

27. (While, Although) the councilman opposed the motion in 2001, he voted for it in 2002.

28. The campaign centers (around, on) civic pride.

29. The *USS Iowa* was (under way, underway) toward the Persian Gulf when the Navy

    ordered it to return to port.

30. The convicted mass murderer was (hanged, hung) at one minute (passed, past) mid-

    night.

31. Mark Twain's house is (a, an) (historic, historical) (cite, sight, site).

32. (A lot, Quite a few, Many) of us were upset because we weren't (contacted, told).

33. We figured that the school's (principle, principal) was our (principle, principal) hope in

    the (stationary, stationery)-run endurance contest.

34. She's (presently, currently) employed by Time and is expecting a big pay (hike, increase).

35. Washington is the (capital, Capitol) of the United States.

36. When the child fell on the sidewalk, she broke her collarbone on the (cement, concrete).

37. The truck (collided with, crashed into) the telephone pole.

38. The United States is (composed of, comprised of, constituted of) 50 states.

39. That book is different (from, than) any other I've read.

40. He was arrested for (drunk, drunken) driving.

41. She's given a (couple, couple of) speeches on abortion.

42. (Hopefully, I hope) it won't snow this week.

43. It's just (as, like) I suspected.

44. What are you trying to (imply, infer) in your article?

45. If three candidates run against each other in an election and the leading candidate wins 40 percent of the vote, that candidate has a (majority, plurality).

CHAPTER 9

Punctuation

Name: _____

Class: _____

Date: _____

Practice: Punctuation

Use proper copy-editing symbols to correct punctuation.

1. Who directed "Return of the Jedi?"

2. Three of her favorite books were "Atlas Shrugged" "Walden", and "Who's Afraid of Virginia Woolf"?

3. Robert Jones, Jr., has worked for Pioneer Foods, Inc. in Carthage Ill. since May 5, 1999 when he substituted for his brother.

4. They had lived in Independence, Kan., Leon, Iowa, and Boulder, Colo.

5. "If it weren't for this teams fighting spirit we wouldn't be No. 1", the coach said.

6. He said, "The U.S. didn't remove Saddam Hussein then, but should have. Then we wouldn't be in this mess today!!!"

7. Suddenly he sprang into action hitting one guard, kicking another, and tripping a third.

8. Stir and let set overnight.

9. Crenna said he'd like that one too.

10. Davies hit the brakes, but couldn't avoid the car.

11. Wong suggested the way to deal with the drug problem was by, "teaching our children early of the dangers."

12. On Friday at Blue Ridge Elementary School a dentist and his staff discussed dental care and teachers used Mr. Gross Mouth to illustrate their points.

13. "The No. 1 problem we're facing is the lack of sufficient state funding", said the dean of the journalism program.

14. Soccer is the most popular sport in most of the world; but it hasn't caught on much in the United States.

15. She loves Thomas Lux's poetry, and enjoys that of Larry Levis also.

16. The poll found seven out of 10 people in the country support the proposal, and another two out of 10 are undecided.

17. She said she thought her daughter was innocent but she was not so certain Strickland was blameless.

18. The researcher said, "We don't think we'll have a cure next week, but we do think this new study could mean a cure sometime down the road. In the meantime, though, I'm afraid a lot of people will suffer."

19. "Why wait till we graduate," asked the student?

20. "Wow!", she said. "I didn't know that."

21. "I think it was the poet Mark Strand who said, "The future isn't what it used to be." the professor said.

22. "I never saw anything like it in my life. And I hope I never do again," she said.

23. "That's a tough call," the coach said. "Let's wait till we see how the next game goes before we start predicting a championship."

   "But I'll tell you this, he added, "I'll be disappointed if we don't take home the trophy."

24. Hacker said about 7,500 deaths in Missouri each year are caused by smoking, and passage of a state law providing clean air indoors is vital for improving public health.

Review: Punctuation

Use proper copy-editing symbols to correct punctuation.

1. He said "It's all rock n roll to me!".

2. She had relatives in Ashland, Mo., Springfield, Ill., and Ottumwa, Iowa.

3. She told the committee, "The U.N. initiatives for more equitable news coverage concerning the Third World have not received much support from the West. Communist countries have been more supportive".

4. He spoke in a slow cheerful manner.

5. In the afternoon three people ran forward, waving their arms, and shouting for him to stop.

6. That is the Smiths' house-the red one.

7. Survivors include two daughters, Carolyn Terry, of Columbia, and Pat Smith of Baltimore, Md., and a brother, Mark Fritz of 1206 W. Broadway.

8. One councilperson disagreed; Pat Barnes, 4th Ward.

9. Seventeen years after he died Rep. Gerald Hawk (R-Ind) was honored by Congress, in a brief 15 minute ceremony.

10. "My face is still slightly swollen after my face lift two weeks ago", she said, "but my doctor says that is normal and I can get my hair done next week."

11. When he graduates in May, Snodgrass says he does not know what he will do.

12. None of the workers required medical treatment, and the leak did not pose a danger to public safety, he said.

13. Hivala said the tribute and activities are for all veterans but the focus is on those in hospitals.

14. Steger said the two communist countries will provide financial and logistical aid, and each will be represented by a member on the six-man expedition crew.

Spelling Relief

Name: _____

Class: _____

Date: _____

Short Answer

1. To check the spelling of a word, what three books should you consult? List them in the order they should be consulted.

2. What is the rule for the order of the letters *i* and *e* in a word?

3. What is the rule for when we typically double the consonant at the end of a word before adding a suffix that starts with a vowel?

Spelling Relief

Name: _____

Class: _____

Date: _____

Practice: Spelling and Hyphenation

Words Often Misspelled

Circle the correct spelling.

1. accommodate, accomodate
2. batallion, battalion
3. cancelation, cancellation
4. cemetary, cemetery
5. concensus, consensus
6. defendant, defendent
7. dietician, dietitian
8. embarass, embarrass
9. employe, employee
10. exagerate, exaggerate
11. fulfill, fullfil
12. guerilla, guerrilla

13. homicide, homocide
14. innocuous, inocuous
15. judgement, judgment
16. kidnaped, kidnapped
17. livable, liveable
18. memento, momento
19. occured, occurred
20. restauranteur, restaurateur
21. separate, seperate
22. seize, sieze
23. totaled, totalled
24. weird, wierd

One Word, Two Words or Hyphenated?

Use proper copy-editing symbols to correct any misspelled words.

1. air conditioner
2. air show
3. alright
4. baby sitter
5. backyard (noun)

6. ball-point pen
7. bestseller (noun)
8. black-board
9. bowlgame
10. carpool

11. CD ROM

12. church-goer

13. copy editor

14. court martialed

15. daylight saving time

16. desk-top

17. dump truck

18. email

19. facelift

20. filmgoers

21. film maker

22. follow-up (adj.)

23. half-brother

24. home owner

25. hot line

26. jet-liner

27. jump shot

28. knick-knack

29. longterm (adj.)

30. long-time (adj.)

31. men's wear

32. midwinter

33. nation-wide

34. non-chalant

35. non-violent

36. one-time (adj.)

37. pot hole

38. powerline

39. pre-election

40. pricetag

41. race track

42. rock-n-roll

43. runningback

44. running-mate

45. schoolbus

46. school teacher

47. sewerline

48. shut-down (noun)

49. shutout (noun)

50. snow man

51. spacewalk

52. sportswriter

53. squeeze play

54. step sister

55. tell-tale

56. tidal wave

57. T shirt

58. toy maker

59. tuneup (noun)

60. video game

Spelling Relief

Name: _____

Class: _____

Date: _____

Review: Spelling and Hyphenation

Words Often Misspelled

Circle the correct spelling in each pair.

1. adviser, advisor

2. compatable, compatible

3. disassociate, dissociate

4. doughnut, donut

5. harass, harrass

6. miniscule, minuscule

7. occasion, occassion

8. parimutual, pari-mutuel

9. supercede, supersede

10. superintendant, superintendent

11. traveled, travelled

12. vice versa, visa versa

One Word, Two Words or Hyphenated?

Use proper copy-editing symbols to correct any misspelled words.

1. all ready

2. back porch

3. bar stool

4. busline

5. by-product

6. chainsaw

7. coffeemaker

8. cover up (noun)

9. day-long

10. floodwaters

11. folksinger

12. freethrow

13. ground rules

14. hair stylist

15. lightbulb

16. lineup (noun)

17. meat loaf

18. miniseries

19. multilateral

20. nametag

21. paperwork

22. peace-keeping

23. pitchout

24. postmortem

25. rightwing (adj.)

26. self esteem

27. semi-finals

28. stepping-stone

29. sweatshirt

30. take-over (noun)

31. teenager

32. underway (not nautical)

33. wind-chill index

CHAPTER 11

Writing as a Journalist

Name: _____

Class: _____

Date: _____

Objectivity and Clarity

A. Label each of these statements *O* if it is objective as defined in journalism, *N* if it is not.

_____ **1.** The pope is infallible.

_____ **2.** God doesn't exist.

_____ **3.** Abortion is murder.

_____ **4.** Businesses don't care about workers.

_____ **5.** The Republican Party believes in limited government, the Democratic Party in big spending.

_____ **6.** Adolf Hitler was a madman.

_____ **7.** The suspect is guilty.

_____ **8.** I think the suspect is guilty.

_____ **9.** He looks guilty.

_____ **10.** The prosecuting attorney contended at the trial the suspect is guilty.

_____ **11.** The candidate looked tired.

_____ **12.** She feels men are all alike, but he believes otherwise.

_____ **13.** It's been so dry here lately, the cows are giving powdered milk.

B. If the story below is accurate and true, what do we know about the statements that follow it in this section? Write *T* if we know a statement to be true, *F* if we know it to be false or *?* if we cannot be sure.

Police are called to the scene of a traffic accident. They find that Sarah Lester's car has collided with a truck owned by Hank Fallon. Lester tells police that she hit the truck when she swerved to miss a child who ran into the street. The driver of the truck says Lester changed lanes and hit him head-on. The police ask him whether he saw a child run into the street, and he says no. Police are unable to locate a child at the scene.

_____ **1.** Sarah Lester made up the story about the child running across the street.

_____ **2.** The police think Lester is lying.

_____ **3.** The truck was driven by Hank Fallon.

_____ **4.** Fallon owned the truck that was totaled.

_____ **5.** Everyone survived the accident.

_____ **6.** We don't know yet whether Lester will get a ticket.

C. Explain briefly any bias in the following sentences.

1. The bureaucrats in the school's student aid department said alumni donations for scholarships are falling short this year.

2. The incumbent refuted his opponent's accusation that he was in the pocket of special-interest groups.

3. She denied the fact that she killed her husband.

4. The City Council still hasn't passed an anti-smoking proposal.

CHAPTER 12
Conciseness

Name: _____

Class: _____

Date: _____

Practice: Tightening Words and Phrases

A. Rewrite, where possible, using single-word verbs rather than phrases.

1. assessed a fine

2. costs the sum of

3. give consideration to

4. make mention of

5. put emphasis on

6. has got to

7. head up

8. gather up

9. hurry up

10. is situated at

11. makes her home

B. Rewrite, where possible, without using *to be* verbs as helping verbs.

1. is representative of

2. will be a participant in

3. it is her intention

C. Rewrite, where possible, using single-word modifiers and connectives rather than phrases.

1. a great deal of

2. all of a sudden

3. off of

4. at this point in time

5. in large measure

6. despite the fact that

7. as a consequence of

8. for the reason that

9. prior to

D. Rewrite, where possible, without redundancies.

1. blazing inferno

2. consensus of opinion

3. fatal killing

4. freewill offering

5. general rule

6. personal friend

7. 12 noon

8. armed gunman

9. blue in color

10. self-confessed

11. completely destroyed

12. whether or not

E. Rewrite, where possible, using simpler, shorter words.

1. amidst

2. coequal

3. contusion

4. effectuate

5. finalize

6. imbibe

7. maximize

8. orientate

9. prioritize

10. residence

11. terminate

12. utilize

Conciseness

Practice: Tightening Sentences

Using proper copy-editing symbols, tighten the following sentences, making sure you don't change the meaning.

1. His use of metaphors is effective.

2. He knew he was weak in the area of grammar.

3. The field of medicine was fascinating to her.

4. The man ran down the street with his briefcase in hand.

5. It was her mind that he admired.

6. After setting a new record, she explained her future plans.

7. A grand total of $5,000 was gathered up.

8. The ball was hit by the catcher.

9. It seems that she is happy.

10. She thought the assignment was an easy one to do.

11. I think that this looks OK to me.

12. There are many who believe otherwise now.

13. It was this book that influenced me the most.

14. In order to get closer to the audience, the speaker stepped off of the stage.

15. The noon luncheon was postponed until later, the chairman said, because past experience told him the new construction would not be entirely completed.

16. The roof was partially destroyed, and the fire chief said a fire could recur again.

17. The professor plans to author his book during the summer months before the fall semester.

18. On two different occasions, the unsolved problem resurfaced again.

19. They are the people who were victims of the Holocaust.

20. The higher court remanded the case back down to the lower court.

21. The accident occurred at 10 p.m. Wednesday night after the driver of the vehicle found his car completely surrounded by a thick fog, he later told police after he hit the tree.

Sexism, Racism and Other "isms"

Name: _____

Class: _____

Date: _____

Short Answer

Your instructor may ask you to write a brief essay on one or more of the following questions.

1. Do journalists edit out insensitive language or stereotypes to be "politically correct" or to be more objective?

2. What role should America's changing demographics play in redefining news values in the 21st century?

3. Are there any "isms" you think journalists should be more aware of that weren't covered in this chapter? What are the major insensitive words and stereotypes often directed against those at the short end of this "ism"?

4. Other than trying to edit out insensitive language and stereotypes, what can be done in a positive way to make news stories more representative of today's realities?

5. If journalists are as liberal as conservatives often say, how do you explain the amount of sexism, racism and other "isms" in the media? Or do you think there really isn't much?

6. When people feel discriminated against, they tend to focus on the effect, whereas those who are doing the discriminating tend to focus on the intent—that is, they're likely to say, "Well, that's not what I meant." Which matters more, effect or intent, when judging whether something is insensitive?

Sexism, Racism and Other "isms"

Name: _____

Class: _____

Date: _____

Practice: Avoiding Offensiveness

Edit or rewrite these sentences to eliminate (1) language that may be offensive to the people involved, (2) language that treats women or minorities unequally to white men or (3) language that excludes people because of sex, race, age, disability and so on.

1. The man charged with rape was defended by a lady lawyer.

2. The mayor was dressed in a gray business suit and pumps as she welcomed the trade delegation.

3. A manager needs to know his people as well as his job.

4. She's a coed at the University of Michigan.

5. Mrs. John (Linda) Ferris, 62, died Oct. 10, 2002, of a heart attack.

6. A man and his wife seem to find it harder these days to stay married.

7. Altobelli is a male secretary at the law firm of Prescott and Heineman.

8. Ms. Smith never married.

9. Thomas Sowell is an eminent black scholar and newspaper columnist.

10. The suspect was described as a Hispanic male of average build in his late teens.

11. A Vietnam veteran held his wife and two children hostage for four hours today in Gary, Ind., before releasing them and committing suicide.

12. A grandmother of three announced Monday that she would run for the City Council.

13. Spend a few hours with Regina Esparza, and her sense of humor is so infectious, you soon forget she's a cripple.

14. She quit work when her child was born and became a housewife.

15. Irishmen have contributed much to this nation.

16. Emily Dickinson is well-thought-of as a poetess.

17. At a garage sale, you can usually Jew the price down below what they're asking.

18. He's still spry at 80.

19. Don't be an Indian giver!

20. After the auto accident, he became a Holy Roller.

21. Janice? She's the woman over there with the butch hair.

22. She's a highly respected actress despite being deaf and dumb.

23. Mankind has been around for at least 100,000 years.

24. Washington doesn't seem to care about the common man and his troubles.

25. Barbara Ohmstead, an attractive blond physician, said she never felt as though she had been discriminated against because she's a woman.

26. Has the garbageman made his pickup yet?

27. Harvard's alumni contribute a great deal to the school.

28. She's a real craftsman in her writing.

CHAPTER 14

Writing News That's Fit for Print

Name: _____

Class: _____

Date: _____

Short Answer

1. In our third approach to picking a lead, what do we say makes the strongest lead of all? What's the next best? What is the fallback position in case neither of those work?

2. What five words describe the basic formula for a hard-news print lead?

3. What are the two kinds of *who* in a lead, and when is each used?

4. What are the four kinds of *what* in a lead, and when is each used?

Name: _____

Class: _____

Date: _____

Practice: Writing News for Print

A. Put a check in front of the people who should receive an immediate-ID lead in a hard-news story in the Springfield News. Base your judgment solely on the description.

_____ **1.** the first lady of the United States

_____ **2.** the mayor of Springfield

_____ **3.** a City Council member

_____ **4.** a rape victim

_____ **5.** Madonna

_____ **6.** a local Navy recruiter

_____ **7.** the head of the local Better Business Bureau

_____ **8.** an assistant professor at Springfield University

_____ **9.** the governor of the state

_____ **10.** the governor of another state, not nearby and not populous

B. How would you write the day or date in describing events taking place on the following days if today is Friday, Nov. 8, 2002?

1. Thursday, Nov. 7, 2002

2. Wednesday, Oct. 23, 2002

3. Tuesday, Nov. 19, 2002

4. Saturday, Nov. 9, 2002

5. Saturday, Jan. 25, 2003

6. Monday, Nov. 4, 2002

7. earlier in the day Friday, Nov. 8, 2002

C. Put a check in front of any of the following leads that suggest a topic instead of stating a thesis. (Ignore lack of time and place information here—they could properly come later because they wouldn't be top priorities in the following stories.)

_____ **1.** The Springfield school board will discuss education at its meeting this Friday.

_____ **2.** A nationally known expert on fire safety lectured the city Fire Department on Thursday about preventing fires in public housing.

_____ **3.** Springfield University researchers said Wednesday they may have isolated a gene responsible for aging.

_____ **4.** The president gave his reasons Friday for cutting taxes.

_____ **5.** The public is invited to sound off to the Springfield Parks Commission this Monday on a proposal to prohibit liquor in the city's parks.

D. Check the story description below that sounds like the best candidate for a summary lead.

_____ The City Council passes a no-smoking-in-public-places ordinance, tables a proposal for a city income tax and agrees with recommendations by the Planning and Zoning Commission to reject two zoning-change requests.

_____ A poll sponsored by ABC shows the president's approval rating has dropped from 68 percent last week to 51 percent this week. A poll sponsored by CBS finds his approval dropped from 65 percent to 53 percent during the same period of time. An NBC poll shows a drop in his approval from 71 percent last week to 59 percent this week.

E. Rewrite the following news items. Make sure that your leads are hard-news leads, that they present information in the best order possible, that they are short and clear but tell everything essential and that they follow wire-service style. These may require more than just one sentence or one paragraph. Assume you are writing the leads for Thursday (Nov. 7) afternoon's Springfield newspaper.

1. On Saturday, Nov. 23, the Springfield Garden Club will hold its regular monthly meeting, at Bill Johnson's house at 1311 Twelfth Street this time, at 12 noon to discuss seed catalogs for spring planting.

2. Bill Knox of Springfield won $14 million in the state lottery in the drawing Nov. 7, 2002. He bought the winning ticket at a neighborhood convenience store Wednesday morning when he stopped in for coffee on his way to work.

3. Thursday morning, the Iraqis launched 10 Scud missiles at Israel. Israeli defense forces shot down all but two with U.S. Patriot missiles. Acting in response to the Iraqis' actions, the president ordered U.S. Navy ships to the area and called allies about re-opening war with Iraq. Iraq gave no reason for the attack and, in fact, denied the attack occurred.

CHAPTER 15

Writing News for Broadcast

Name: _____

Class: _____

Date: _____

Short Answer

A. What are the six main differences between writing news for broadcast and writing news for print?

B. Mark each of the following statements *T* if true or *F* if false.

_____ 1. Broadcast news often allows more leeway for expressing personal judgments, especially if noncontroversial.

_____ 2. Broadcast news stories often begin with a general statement that would probably be edited out if run in a newspaper.

_____ 3. Because broadcast stories are so short, no information should ever be repeated.

_____ 4. Broadcast writers must be more aware of homonyms than print writers.

_____ 5. Most experts agree that good grammar and spelling are of little importance in writing broadcast news.

_____ 6. Every print news lead should include *who, what, when, where, why* and *how*.

_____ 7. Print stories can use the time element *yesterday* or *tomorrow* but never *this morning, this afternoon, this evening* or *tonight*.

_____ 8. *Time, day* or *date* should rarely, if ever, start a lead.

_____ 9. Broadcasters are more likely than print journalists to put the attribution at the end of a sentence.

_____ 10. Broadcasters generally prefer present tense even in hard-news stories.

_____ 11. Broadcast sentences tend to be a bit longer than print sentences because they have to get in more information in a shorter period of time.

_____ 12. A question lead should be used only when the question will be answered in the story.

_____ 13. Clichés make great leads and snappers because everyone identifies with them.

_____ 14. Differing advice between print and broadcast classes often has to do with differences in the nature of the media.

Name: _____

Class: _____

Date: _____

Practice: Broadcast Style

Rewrite the following items in broadcast style.

1. 17 cents

2. $33

3. 75 percent

4. FBI

5. Mister

6. NAACP

7. NATO

8. Interstate 66

9. 33 billion

10. 4.5 trillion

11. 1 1/2

12. score of three to one

13. 1608 W. Elm

14. the year 1996

15. Dow Jones index down three points

16. May 31

CHAPTER 16

Writing for the Online Media

Name: _____

Class: _____

Date: _____

Short Answer

1. Some people believe the online media will endanger democratic societies by allowing the public to read only the news it wants to read, thereby lessening understanding of critical public issues. Explain why you agree or disagree with this theory.

2. Unlike the traditional media, the online media have virtually unlimited space because news and other information are called from computerized databases on demand. Describe how you would help consumers sort through this mass of information.

3. Compare the CNN Web site to the USA Today Web site on the same day. Describe differences in their approach to delivering the news online.

4. If you were assigned the task of creating a Web site for a newspaper, what innovative features would you use to ensure local appeal? Describe how you would make your site different from those of other area newspapers.

5. Using the criteria outlined in this chapter, analyze the Web site of your college newspaper for credibility. If your newspaper does not have such a Web site, choose that of another college.

6. Examine the USA Today Web site, and describe how it uses the technique of layering in the presentation of news. Be specific in your analysis.

Short Answer

Mark each of the following statements *T* if true or *F* if false. In addition to the appendix, consult the index of "Working With Words" and your wire-service stylebook for information.

_____ 1. Initials of three letters or more almost always take periods.

_____ 2. With the names of specific plants, animals and foods, capitalize only the proper noun. For example: *red delicious apple, German shepherd, English muffin.*

_____ 3. When products have become so well-known that many people use their names generically — such as *Band-Aid, Dumpster, Jell-O, Kitty Litter* and *Styrofoam* — lowercase them so as not to give the products a free ad.

_____ 4. Question marks and exclamation points can go inside or outside quotation marks at the end of a sentence depending on whether they are part of the quote.

_____ 5. Don't put a comma before the word *and* in a series or the abbreviation *Inc.* or *Jr.,* but do put a comma after a state when it follows a city or after a year when it follows a date.

_____ 6. In the phrase "well-prepared student," *well* and *prepared* are coordinate adjectives.

_____ 7. To find out how a word is spelled, look it up first in the AP Stylebook. If it's not there, look it up next in Webster's New World College Dictionary. If it's not there, look it up in Webster's Third New International Dictionary.

_____ 8. Journalists write about events using the date-time-place formula. For example: *The event will take place Jan. 31 at noon at McKenney Union.*

_____ 9. Journalists do not use the word *yesterday* or *tomorrow.* Instead, they use the name of the day of the week.

_____ 10. The numbers zero through nine are usually written out; 10 and up are written as numerals.

_____ 11. Official titles, such as *president* or *mayor,* are capitalized only if they precede a person's name.

_____ 12. Newspapers still typically use courtesy titles such as *Mr.* and *Mrs.*

_____ 13. Months with five or fewer letters are never abbreviated.

_____ 14. Of the words *avenue, boulevard, circle, drive, highway, lane* and *street,* only *avenue, boulevard* and *street* are abbreviated with a street address.

_____ **15.** The eight states that are never abbreviated are Alabama, Hawaii, Missouri, Utah, Tennessee, Iowa, Idaho and Oregon.

_____ **16.** Put a comma between compound modifiers.

_____ **17.** Always put a comma after a month.

_____ **18.** Either use commas around an address or use the word *of* in front of the address, without commas around the address.

_____ **19.** The words *million, billion* and *trillion* are normally written out with a numeral in front of them.

_____ **20.** The city in a dateline is written in all capital letters, but the state or country is not.

Name: _____

Class: _____

Date: _____

Practice: Wire-Service Style

Abbreviations and Acronyms

Circle the correct answers.

1. 6 AM, 6 a.m.

2. AM radio, a.m. radio

3. 1492 A.D., A.D. 1492

4. 300 B.C., B.C. 300

5. t.v. set, TV set

6. cable television, cable TV

7. United Nations observer, U.N. observer

8. the United States, the U.S.

9. Washington, D.C.; Washington

10. New York, New York City

11. CIA, C.I.A.

12. NATO, N.A.T.O.

13. FBI, F.B.I.

14. COD, c.o.d.

15. eight percent, 8 percent

16. $.25, 25 cents

17. September 2002, Sept. 2002

18. Fri., Jun. 14, 2002; June 14, 2002

19. October 9, Oct. 9

20. Christmas vacation, Xmas vacation

21. Fourth of July parade, July 4 parade

22. Reverend Al Sharpton, the Rev. Al Sharpton

23. Prof. Martin Shichtman, Professor Martin Shichtman

24. Representative John Dingell (D-MI); Rep. John Dingell, D, Mich.

25. Pres. George W. Bush's Cabinet, President George W. Bush's Cabinet

26. National Organization for Women (NOW), National Organization for Women

27. Acme Company, Inc.; Acme Co. Inc.

28. Computer Company of America, Computer Co. of America

29. 101 Wisteria Dr., 101 Wisteria Drive

30. 10th St., Tenth Street

31. U.S. Highway 23 S., U.S. Highway 23 South

32. Maple Ave., Maple Avenue

33. 1220 Main Street East, 1220 Main St. E.

34. Interstate 94, I-94 [first reference]

35. Fort Worth, Texas; Ft. Worth, Texas

36. Detroit; Detroit, MI

37. We're number one, We're No. 1

38. OK, okay

39. Brown v. Board of Education, Brown vs. Board of Education

Capitalization

A. Use proper copy-editing symbols to fix any capitalization problems.

1. Red Delicious Apple

2. german shepherd

3. french fries

4. basset hound

5. lily of the valley

6. Boston cream pie

7. styrofoam

8. kleenex

9. Kitty Litter

10. fiberglass

11. sheetrock

12. realtor

B. Use proper copy-editing symbols to fix any capitalization problems.

1. South Korea

2. Eastern United States

3. southern accent

4. a western (movie)

5. Drive two miles north.

6. out west

7. southeast Michigan

8. South Side of Chicago

C. Use proper copy-editing symbols to fix any capitalization problems.

1. Pioneer and Huron High Schools

2. Detroit and Huron rivers

D. Use proper copy-editing symbols to fix any capitalization problems.

1. Psychology Department

2. English department

3. state department

4. the fire department

5. Springfield police

6. tax committee

7. Master's degree

8. President's cabinet

9. Board of Directors

10. Massachusetts Legislature

11. City Council

12. Democratic Party

13. communist philosophy

14. socialist ideas

E. Use proper copy-editing symbols to fix any capitalization problems.

1. "Let us praise him [God] in prayer."

2. The pope said mass.

3. The priest offered communion to the congregation.

F. Use proper copy-editing symbols to fix any capitalization problems.

1. black

2. caucasian

3. Native American

G. Use proper copy-editing symbols to fix any capitalization problems.

1. Mayor Michael Bloomberg

2. Cowboy Roy Rogers

Numbers

Circle the correct answers.

1. 1213 Eleventh St., 1213 11th St.

2. 6-day-old baby, six-day-old baby

3. Apollo XI, Apollo 11

4. three cents, 3 cents

5. score of 3-2, score of three to two

6. 3rd Ward, Third Ward

7. temperature of −3, temperature of minus 3

8. 1/2, one-half

9. 1 1/2, one and one-half

10. 1st Amendment, First Amendment

11. 2 million, two million

12. Nineteen-sixty-eight was a great year. 1968 was a great year.

13. Five percent of the solution is left. 5 percent of the solution is left.

14. seven pounds, two ounces; 7 pounds, 2 ounces

15. six feet tall, 6 feet tall

16. 9:00 a.m., 9 a.m.

17. 2 hours, two hours

18. the 1990's, the 1990s

19. 3rd Congressional District, Third Congressional District

20. 11, eleven

21. Air Force One, Air Force 1

22. 5 mph, five mph

23. 9-yard run, nine-yard run

24. 3 under par, three under par

25. 9th Street, Ninth Street

26. 1st Lt. Rene Walten, First Lt. Rene Walten

27. 8, eight

Wire-Service Style Summary

Name: _____

Class: _____

Date: _____

Review: Wire-Service Style

Use proper copy-editing symbols to edit these sentences only for AP style or errors. Otherwise, do not rewrite them.

1. The FBI (Federal Bureau of Investigation) and the C.I.A. have all ready agreed on anti-terrorist procedures.

2. Anderson graduated in 1978 with a masters in science and he is now a History Professor at Northwestern University.

3. She lives at 1,457 Washington Rd., and is trying to effect a City council decision that would allow her to co-own the place.

4. W.E.M.U. has been upgraded during recent months and is on the verge of a "great, new era," the Chairman of the Communications Department at E.M.U. said.

5. Coach Ed Thorpe praised Assistant Coach Jimmy Giles but Thorpe ignored the other Coaches Harrison, Manis, Jordan and Martin.

6. The battered quarterback said, "Its hard being a superstar all of the time. It was a dark terrible day out there today.

7. More snow was forecasted for later this week, but accumulations were not expected to accede five inches by November 5th.

8. The Mississippi river was one of the keys to victory for the north during the Civil War.

9. Martin Luther King day is celebrated officially here at the University with a holiday.

10. The judgment called for I-70 to be widened and improved East of Arrow Rock, MO.

11. Harry J, Johnson, Jr. was elected Gov. over the opposition of some Police Departments.

12. Jesus's message was to spread His Gospel to all the world, said Rev. Ben Steele.

13. He said he could have made a $200-million dollar deal if he'd seen the opportunity ahead of time.

14. Eleven freshman joined the class on the 1st day, increasing the class size by eight percent.

15. The President was sitting in the oval office while a member of the Palestinian delegation lectured about 35 persons outside the White House about Democracy.

16. The principle estimated a student-teacher ratio of 18 to 1 at Wilson High School.

17. 2000 ranked as one of the hottest summers on record locally; but normal winter weather was expected.

18. The kids enrolled in the kindergarten class at Mt. Shasta School range in age from 18mos. to five year olds.

19. Senator Christopher Bond, a republican from Missouri, spoke at Commencement.

20. Thousands of persons from Southeast Michigan are expected to attend the fair which has been okayed to start Nov. 4.

21. The History Department elected Ass. Prof. Harold Burgraf their new chairman.

22. Grant Forman, Director of the agriculture office here, said the plant is part of a ten-million dollar effort to upgrade assistance to local farmers.

23. R.P. Watson, Jr., 56 was chosen Pres. from among twenty candidates at the Board meeting Feb. 16.

24. The girl is 6-years-old, but the race is only for 5 year olds.

25. The man, in his 30's, has a daughter two-months old.

26. Frank Smith, former Prof. of Business Administration at Syracuse, is mayor of the City of New Orleans.

27. The National Organization for Women (NOW) will celebrate their anniversary at a meeting October 13 at 602 West Boulevard.

28. Washtenaw and Wayne Counties were singled out for lottery promotions.

29. Anthony Hines has a B.A. degree from the University of Texas at Austin, an M.A. degree from Ohio State University, and a doctorate degree from the Massachusetts Institute of Technology.

30. Springfield's Fire Chief said the city's fire department was better able to fight fires because of state grants.

31. The city council decided last night to postpone spending $135 thousand on a fire engine to replace one damaged in a December, 2001, accident that killed Springfield fireman, Donald Crum.

32. Ray Hamburger, City Manager, gave the okay to take various funds from the budget, and the Council voted 6-to-2 to approve the plan.

33. The "Springfield News" has found that Springfield policemen are entitled to a two-and-a-half percent pay hike for 15-hours of college credit.

34. If convicted on the charge of 1st degree murder, he faces 7 years in jail without probation.

35. "The Federal Government's roll in this is limited", said the ex. Sen. on Fox News Channel's The O'Reilly Factor.

36. Representative Paul Dawson (Dem.-Springfield) is one of a handful of state Legislators who has announced their retirement after this session.

37. The budget cuts in the Department represent a 3 year city plan to faze out some of it's services.

38. The Springfield School Board will meet tomorrow at 2:00 P.M. in the afternoon.

39. Basketball season is just around the corner and the Cocahes at Springfield and Central High Schools couldn't be happier.

40. The class concentrated on its number one problem: Spelling.

41. Dr. William Spence asked everyone in the Philosophy Department to pay twenty scents for each cup of coffee.

42. The Springfield City Prosecutor dropped all charges Monday against 17 protestors arrested on the University Campus Wednesday, October 21.

43. The Springfield police department will be out in force when the cabinet member and the Pope meet August 2nd.

44. The White House said Monday it was happy about the House's vote of 302 to 132.

45. The United Nations session will get under way with a debate on the topic of free trade versus protectionism.

46. The temperature fell by noon to –10.

47. Temperatures Thursday were in the '30's.

Name: _____

Class: _____

Date: _____

Use proper copy-editing symbols to edit this story.

Collectors of handcrafted art and clothing will be thrilled with the abundance of goods on display this weekend at Springfield's First Annual Crafts Show.

Over 220 artists from Michigan and as far away as Kentucky will be on hand to display their wares. Items range from ceramics and woodwork to needlepoint, dolls and appliqued clothing.

The show runs from 11 a.m. to 5 p.m. Sun., Jan. 31 at the Springfield Arts Center. No admission.

So come on out, have fun, and support your local artists and craftsmen.

Use proper copy-editing symbols to edit this story.

The Springfield Planning and Zoning Commission is seeking citizen input this Thursday on if it should allow a Wal-Mart to be built in the Bensonhurst section of town.

Wal-mart is seeking Commission approval to change the zoning status for the neighborhood from residential only to residential and commercial to allow building the store.

Commissioners voted at their last meeting to hold a public hearing on the matter. The Commission said they want to get citizen's reaction to the idea, especially from those who live in that area of town.

Commissioner Fatima Schwartz said she worried if the increased traffic to the quiet neighborhood would bother residents. Commissioner Peter Hendrickson said he wondered if downtown merchants wouldn't be upset at the possible loss of business as well as full-time jobs to Wal-Mart's part-time employee pool.

However, Commissioner Ann Overhouse said she thought the people of Springfield would appreciate the lower prices, greater variety, and extra jobs that approval of the store would mean.

The commission will meet at the County-City Building Tuesday at 7 PM..

Story Editing

Name ____________________

Class ____________________

Date ____________________

Story Editing: Obituary

Name: _____

Class: _____

Date: _____

Use proper copy-editing symbols to edit this story.

Oscar C. Pemboldt, 1311 Maplewood Dr. met his Maker Sunday, Feb. 6, 2002 at Springfield Memorial Hospital. He was 81.

Pemboldt, a press operator for the Springfield News for thirty years was born November 3, 1921 in Manchester to William and Henrietta Pemboldt.

He married Annette Evers June 13, 1943. The couple resided in Springfield for 55 years where they attended Springfield Community United Methodist Church. She preceded him in death in 1998.

He is survived by two daughters: Virginia L. Graham, of 1908 Westview Rd., and Alberta Huxley, Toledo, Ohio; a son Greg Pemboldt, Detroit, and two grandchildren.

Visitation will be 7 AM to 9 p.m. at Springfield Funeral Home, 15300 South Adams. Funeral services will be conducted by Rev. David C. Collins at 11 a.m. Saturday at the funeral home. Burial will be at Ridgewood Cemetary, 948 N. River afterwards.

Name: _____

Class: _____

Date: _____

Use proper copy-editing symbols to edit this story.

Wednesday, Dr. Sarah Farmer, an astronomy professor at Springfield University, and an expert in the search for intelligent life in the galaxy, spoke at the meeting of the Springfield Science Fiction Club.

Dr. Farmer said that probably 10 per cent of stars probably have planetary systems. Scientists have detected radio signals originating from beyond the solar system with super computers.

Though these so far seem routine, Farmer said, "she's optimisitic that signals will eventually be found that will give us the first hint of life on other planets".

Likewise, she said because of the great distances involved, planets circling the closest stars could be receiving the signals from Earth's first TV broadcasts about now.

"It's possible extraterrestrials could sense patterns in our TV signals indicating intelligence and amplify and decode them."

That means ET's could now be enjoying the original broadcasts of shows like "I Love Lucy." I wonder what will they think when they eventually get "Star Trek?"

Story Editing: Speech Story

Name:

Class:

Date:

Use [illegible] editing [illegible] story.

Wednesday, Dr. Sarah Palmer, astronomy professor at [illegible] and an expert on the search for intelligent life in the universe, spoke [illegible] Springfield [illegible] Club.

Dr. Palmer said [illegible] "[illegible] are [illegible] [illegible] have detected [illegible] beyond [illegible] signal [illegible]"

"[illegible]," Palmer said, "[illegible] [illegible] life [illegible] planet."

[illegible] because of the great distances involved [illegible] from [illegible] TV [illegible]

"It's [illegible] [illegible] [illegible]

"[illegible] the original [illegible] I Love Lucy [illegible] when they eventually [illegible] Star Trek [illegible]

Name: _____

Class: _____

Date: _____

Use proper copy-editing symbols to edit this story.

Police say they've solved a string of 5 campus-area sexual assaults with the arrest of William Gilbert Thursday for attempted rape. Claudia Frank, 510 High Street, apt. 206, said she was wakling home from Ellis Library about 7 p.m. Thursday night when Gilbert jumped from a bush outside her building and attempted to pull her to the ground.

But Frank apparently didn't know his intended victim was tough as she is good looking. At 36, she's still a stunner: tall, blonde and beautiful. And she's a stunner in another sense: She has a black belt in karate.

When police arrived within minutes of a phone call from her, they found her would-be rapist's ardor considerably cooled: Gilbert's "victim" had kneed him in the groin, broken his nose with a thrust of her palm, and snapped his kneecap with a kick. Police said Gilbert was writhing in pain ehrn thry arrived and shouted to them: "I'll give you a confesion, what ever you want! Just get her away from me!"

He was listed in satisfactory condition Thrusday night at Boone County Hospital.

One unnamed police officer said, "He's lucky she didn8t kill him. Here's a jerk that's sent several women to the hospital. Now the tables are turned. It couldn't have happpened to a nicer guy.

Use proper copy-editing symbols to edit this story.

Most professional women have a better relationship with their pets then there husbands or children; and more than half say their under too much stress and want more time. According to a survey of women in the work place by Young & Rubicam.

48 per cent of women consider themselves "cash rich and time poor." Amongst these women, if given the option of having a 10 per cent hike in either salary or free time, 61 percent would forego extra cash for more time.

But when asked to rate their satisfaction with hubby, children, work colleagues, and friends, the winner was; pets. Though women place more importance on their relationships with various humans in their lives, the only relationship a majority of women (54 percent) rated as 'very satisfying' was with a feline or canine. Children were second, with that relationship "very satisfying to 50% of women surveyed.

Not surprisingly given today's societies impossible schedules, 51 percent of women reported having too much stress in their lives. And if they had a choice between having an exiting career or a simple life, 49 percent would chose the later, 43 percent of respondants would option for a high powered career over a simple life and 11 per cent even claim they thrive on stress.